Personal
Best

THE NATIONAL BUSINESS EMPLOYMENT WEEKLY PREMIER GUIDES SERIES

<u>Published:</u>

Resumes, Second Edition,	ISBN# 0-471-15648-5 paper
Interviewing, Second Edition,	ISBN# 0-471-15646-9 paper
Cover Letters, Second Edition,	ISBN# 0-471-15649-3 paper
Networking,	ISBN# 0-471-31026-3 cloth; ISBN# 0-471-31027-1 paper
Jobs Rated Almanac,	ISBN# 0-471-05495-X paper
Love Your Work,	ISBN# 0-471-11956-3 paper
Self-Employment,	ISBN# 0-471-10918-5 paper
Personal Best: 1001 Great Career Ideas for Achieving Success in Your Career,	ISBN# 0-471-14888-1 paper

Personal
Best

1001 Great Ideas for
Achieving Success
in Your Career

Joe Tye with

John Wiley & Sons, Inc.

New York • Chichester • Brisbane • Toronto • Singapore • Weinheim

This text is printed on acid-free paper.

Copyright © 1997 by National Business Employment Weekly
Published by John Wiley & Sons, Inc.

Library of Congress Cataloging-in-Publication Data:

Tye, Joe.
    Personal best : 1001 great ideas for achieving success in your
career / by Joe Tye:
National Business Employment Weekly
        p.   cm. — (The National business employment weekly premier
guides series)
    Includes bibliographical references
    ISBN 0-471-14888-1 (pbk. : alk. paper)
    1. Career development.   2. Success.   I. National
business employment weekly.   II. Title.   III. Series.
HF5381.T93   1996
650.1—dc20   96-20398

Printed in the United States of America

10 9 8 7 6 5 4 3 2 1

ACKNOWLEDGMENTS

Thanks to all of the dedicated career professionals and authors who helped me collect the ideas and case studies included in this book, as well as the many people who shared their own stories. In particular, *The National Business Employment Weekly* and the Outplacement Institute's *Excellence In Outplacement Practice,* edited by James J. Gallagher, were invaluable.

I wish I could single out all of the people who spent time on the telephone with me, but those who went above and beyond the call of duty include Mary S. Murphy, Arlene Hirsch, Mary Jane Murphy, Jim Kacena, Doug Richardson, Joan Lloyd, Ray Cech, Monika Freidel, Dan Burrus, Pat Plemmons, Jim Heuerman, Martin Groder, Jane Wessman, Linda Kline, Arlynn Greenbaum, Sheridan Stolarz, Ed Myers, and Jim Gallagher. A number of publishers provided review copies of career and business books, and I especially want to acknowledge the generosity of John Wiley & Sons, VGM, and Ten Speed Press. And thanks to Tom Cheney for his terrific cartoons.

Burt Dubin and Dottie Walters have been of tremendous support in my speaking career, and literary agents Faith Hamlin and Michael Larsen have taught me much about the publishing business. I owe an unpayable debt of gratitude to everyone who read my first book, *Never Fear, Never Quit: A Story of Courage and Perseverance* and encouraged me to keep working at getting this important message out.

My wife Sally and daughter Annie typed the manuscript, while son Doug worked hard to help me keep a perspective on what's really important in life. In closing the acknowledgments of the book *Never Fear, Never Quit,* I commented that in my research to develop Ten Eternal Principles for Success and Happiness, "it struck me that the most pervasive theme in all this wisdom is that real success and happiness *requires* spiritual faith in the transcendent meaning of life and submission to the will of a higher power." I believe that now more than ever and am grateful to God for the friends who have come into my life and for the opportunities to be a friend to others.

This book is dedicated to Tony Lee, Editor in Chief of the *National Business Employment Weekly*. Tony's integrity, energy, and genuine concern for people represent the highest qualities to which anyone in the business of helping others achieve career success and personal happiness should aspire.

ABOUT THE AUTHOR

Joe Tye is founder of Paradox 21 in Solon, Iowa. Paradox 21 produces publications, seminars, and products that promote the theme of self-empowerment through faith and action.

Prior to founding Paradox 21, Tye spent 20 years in health care administration, where he was chief operating officer for two large East Coast teaching hospitals. He founded STAT (Stop Teenage Addiction to Tobacco), which is dedicated to protecting children from the tobacco industry. Joe earned a masters degree in health care administration from the University of Iowa and an M.B.A. from the Stanford University Graduate School of Business. He serves on the graduate adjunct faculty at the University of Iowa. His books include *Never Fear, Never Quit: A Story of Courage and Perseverance, Staying on Top When the World's Upside Down,* and *The Self-Transformation Workbook*. He has also produced several audio and videotape programs, including "Success Warrior: Applying the 12 Principles of Military Strategy to Business, Career, and Sales Success." In addition to frequent speaking and seminar engagements, he organizes Never Fear, Never Quit conferences around the country.

CONTENTS

INTRODUCTION

There are a ton of career books out there. I know, because I've read most of them. There are some that are truly outstanding, a great number that are pretty good, and some that constitute either editorial or career counseling malpractice. So does the world need another career book?

Yes. *1001 Great Career Ideas* is unique and special in several ways. First, you don't have to read it from cover to cover to benefit from it; just open it to the chapter covering the subject you're most interested in, and you'll find some great ideas that you can immediately apply to your situation.

Second, though it's in a "bullet" format, it's not a superficial "Eat Your Wheaties" type of book; a great deal of research and thought has gone into assuring that the information is practical, helpful, and proven.

Third, the book is comprehensive, so no matter where you are in your career planning or job search, you're certain to find lots of ideas that will help you. Pull it off your bookshelf six months from now, when your circumstances may have changed, and you'll find lots of other ideas that are relevant to your new situation.

Fourth, though some information, particularly that dealing with electronic job search, becomes quickly dated, most of the ideas in this book are timeless. And, finally, because this book reflects my firm belief that emotional and spiritual skills are more important to your long-range career success than practical and technical skills, many of these Great Ideas are for the right side of your brain—the side where the poet, dancer, lover, and dreamer resides inside of you.

It never ceases to amaze me how many good ideas there are in the world—that particular well never runs dry! It won't be long before we'll need to write *1001 More Great Career Ideas*. If you'd like to contribute your ideas, please write to me:

Joe Tye
Paradox 21
P.O. Box 480
Solon, IA 52333-0480

1

Self-Assessment
and Self-Knowledge

*The world of work ain't what it used to be. The long-held
contract between employers and employees has been ruptured.
Since we can no longer rely on "the company" for security, it
must come from within. For people who know who they are and
what they're called to do, it will be a world of great opportunity.
For those who continue to define themselves in terms of the
expectations and opinions of others, it will be a world of pain
and frustration.*

*More often than not we don't want to know ourselves, don't want
to depend on ourselves, don't want to live with ourselves. By middle life, most of us are accomplished fugitives from ourselves.*

John W. Gardner, *Self-Renewal*

King Solomon began the book of Proverbs by stating that a
wise person will hear and increase learning, and that a person of understanding will seek wise counsel. At about the same
time, but on the other side of the earth, Lao Tzu said that one who
knows others is wise, while one who knows oneself is enlightened.

Self-awareness is a continuous, lifelong process of learning and introspection.

Here are some things that you can do to help discover who you are and what you should set about to do:

1. Write an autobiography.

2. Keep a daily journal, including a description of your thoughts and emotions.

3. Take time every day for peaceful meditation.

4. Pay attention in the course of every day to those things that you find rewarding and enjoyable, and those that you do not.

5. Every day critique your own performance against the internal standards that you establish.

6. Ask others what they think your ideal job or your calling might be.

7. Seek outside help from counselors or testing services.

The question I struggled with for many years goes something like this: How can I keep my life and my work properly separated? It was the wrong question. The right question . . . is: How can I keep my life and my work properly integrated?

James A. Autry, *Life and Work*

What's your primary purpose or mission in life? Who are you really trying to become? It takes courage to concentrate your resources effectively on this priority, because of all you must do without. But it's also the only way that you'll accomplish anything of real significance.

Without having your own personal mission statement as bedrock, you'll never really buy into any organization's mission statement. Without buying into the organization's mission statement, you'll never really feel a part of it, and never really be successful. It took me nearly two years to write my own personal mission statement. Now, however, it has been a tremendous asset for helping me focus my time and energy on key priorities, and saying "no" to tempting diversions that don't really contribute to what I want to accomplish in the long run in both my professional and my personal life. This is my personal mission statement:

> My mission is—through my personal example and my work—to: (1) help organizations achieve quantum leaps in creativity and productivity by teaching people the practical, emotional, and spiritual skills of personal empowerment; and (2) help individuals create personal meaning and fulfillment through their work, and live their lives with courage and perseverance.

Don't wait around for someone to empower you, because it will never happen. The only person who can empower you will be the one sitting around waiting to be empowered.

Self-mastery calls for thorough familiarity with one's mental and emotional strengths. And it calls for sustaining a commitment to personal growth—the understanding of what makes you tick as an individual—as well as professional development.

Charles Garfield, *Peak Performers*

Joseph Imburgia, president of Diagnostic Sciences in Chicago, suggests that you ask yourself the following questions to determine whether you are a good candidate for vocational testing to clarify your skills, interests, values, and personality style:

1. Do you need to have things spelled out in detail before you are comfortable making a decision?

2. Is it difficult for you to express your career interests and personal strengths?

3. Do you tend to be impulsive and make rash decisions?

4. Do your career interests tend to fluctuate, making it hard for you to know what you want to do?

5. Do you feel overwhelmed by information and long to have it organized more effectively to help in your decision making?

If you answered "yes" to any of these questions, vocational testing might help you clarify your aptitudes, interests and goals.

Should you take any of the various self-assessment tools to help you understand your personality, skills, or aptitudes? Diane Goldner, a New York writer, took the Campbell Interest and Skill Survey and the Myers-Briggs Type Indicator test which suggested a number of possible suitable careers. Among others, both indicated she'd make a good writer. Perhaps, she concludes, there's a value in getting a second or third opinion that confirms your self-knowledge.

Great speakers constantly work on ways to improve their performances. They don't think of any of their work as difficult. Every aspect is pleasure because they love speaking so much.

Dottie Walters and Lilly Walters, *Speak and Grow Rich*

Career counselor Margo Frey, president of Career Development Services of Milwaukee, tells of a person who used the Myers-Briggs tool to help her on her job. She was on the production end of an advertising firm, and constantly frustrated at being stuck between the demands of the creative department and its endless ideas, and management with its pressures to finalize product. She couldn't understand why people simply couldn't keep working together to get the job done. After going through the Myers-Briggs, the woman discovered that she hadn't properly understood her role vis-à-vis the creative department and management, and the types of personalities attracted to each function.

The new economy will be a service economy. No matter what you make or do on the job, evaluate yourself as a "servant." How well do you serve your "customers," and what can you do to become better?

An important part of knowing yourself is constantly improving yourself. Humans are in constant change, and it requires deliberate effort to assure that the change is in a positive direction. Chart a plan for the knowledge that you need or want to have, and then stick to it.

There's paradox in all life, not the least of which is knowing which of your personal values to follow when they come into conflict. Harold Grinspoon is both a successful entrepreneur as founder of Aspen Square Management Co. in West Springfield, Massachusetts, and a generous philanthropist. Having built his business in the tough commercial and multifamily real estate market, he has had to learn when to be tough according to the requirements of the business and when to be generous in accord with his inner nature. A further paradox: his being tough in business has now allowed him to be a much bigger giver to charitable causes. Like the song says, "you gotta know when to hold 'em, and know when to fold 'em."

There's a persistent belief that "nice guys finish last." Not only do they not finish last, but they ultimately finish at or near the top, while the "bad guys" consistently finish behind the 8-ball, behind bars, or near the bottom.

Zig Ziglar (from the foreword to *On My Honor, I Will* by Randy Pennington and Marc Bockmon)

You may have read that you should be tightly focused, that the time for the Renaissance Man was during the Renaissance. Consider, however, that we are living in a new Renaissance, and that learning as broadly as possible will enhance your creativity.

George Valliant, a Harvard University psychologist, followed a group of Harvard graduates for more than three decades. He found that those with a better sense of humor, which he measured by assigning a value for HQ, for humor quotient, were healthier, wealthier and more likely to be promoted, than their humor-challenged compatriots. After you've read sports and business, turn to the comics; learn a new joke every week.

There's an age-old debate about what must come first: a change in your attitude or a change in your behavior. Why take a chance? If something in your life is not working satisfactorily, change both, starting right now.

Read the book *Act Now!* by Dale L. Anderson, M.D. Building upon the scientific evidence of a strong mind-body connection, Anderson describes how you can use acting techniques to break bad habits, build good habits and improve your attitude. Your success at accomplishing this, he says, will dramatically improve your health, wealth and relationships. All the world's a stage, said the bard, so why not write your own script?

I cannot stress too much the need for self-invention. To be authentic is literally to be your own author . . . to discover your own native energies and desires, and then to find your own way of acting on them.

Warren Bennis, *On Becoming A Leader*

Mary Jane Murphy, a career counselor and psychotherapist in Atlanta, says that about 30 percent of the people she sees end up with at least a brief period of psychotherapy before plunging into the job search. There is, she says, often a pattern of failure showing up in work and personal life, causing them to repeat the same tragic mistakes. If your career has hit the rocks, consider whether a period of self-evaluation might help you avoid a replay in the future.

Wendell Hall quit General Motors after being asked to move for the thirteenth time in 31 years. In assessing his own skills and interests, he realized that he loved the process of buying and selling homes in all those moves. He earned a real estate license and started at the bottom of that profession. Now, 10 years later, he owns a real estate brokerage firm—Prudential Lambert Real Estate Inc.—in Oakland, New Jersey, and employs dozens of sales associates. He enjoys both the work and the fact that he's directly rewarded—via commissions—for his performance.

Kerry Bunker, an associate of the Center for Creative Leadership in Greensboro, North Carolina, tells of a bright executive who used self-knowledge to his own benefit. He learned that he was a highly controlling person, and that this tendency alienated his colleagues. He turned his controlling tendencies on himself, controlling his controlling tendencies. He stopped looking so closely over shoulders, and started keeping a daily journal to monitor his own progress. He became more comfortable with letting go, even if it meant output of lower quality than if he'd done it himself. And he paradoxically found his career progressing more smoothly and rapidly.

From a purely selfish standpoint, [improving yourself] is a lot more profitable than trying to improve others.

　　　　　Dale Carnegie, *How to Win Friends and Influence People*

Sometimes the best way to find yourself is to get lost. P.B. Walsh was a college professor and forensic therapist at a maximum security prison in Pennsylvania. She took a week-long retreat at a hermitage cabin in New Mexico where she was totally out of touch. She loved the solitude so much that she moved to remote rural Colorado, down a dirt road 16 miles from the nearest town.

Rick Klump suffered what might be the ultimately deflating job loss; after seven years at a seminary, he was told that he wasn't cut out for the monastic life and had to leave. He went through a period of intense anger, and received counseling for a number of years. Finally, he came back to the church, made many new friends, and riveted his attention on all that he has to be thankful for. He loves his job as a cab driver in St. Louis, shares a nice home with his wife, and is putting his children through good schools. Gratitude, he says, changed his life.

Stacy Feldman, a counselor with The Five O'Clock Club, a national job-search support group based in New York City, suggests doing what you wear. The "uniform" often identifies a person by industry (blue collar) or by company (IBM's white shirts versus Apple's blue jeans). Consider the wardrobe you have and what you like to wear in targeting your best occupation, company, or geographic location.

We learn best when we are learning about ourselves, when we're discovering truths that speak of inner and outer realities, when we're finding out what makes us unique—and like others— within the community.

Marsha Sinetar, *To Build the Life You Want,*
Create the Work You Love

Ellen J. Wallach, a Seattle consultant specializing in career and organizational development, says you need to make your own luck by:

▶ Challenging assumptions.

▶ Recognizing opportunities.

▶ Using the chance to take advantage of the unexpected. (Don't procrastinate when opportunity presents itself!)

▶ Taking risks.

▶ Building networks.

Allen Grossman is Executive Director of Outward Bound. Having moved from a highly successful family business into the nonprofit world, his eyes may point to the stars, but his feet are firmly on the ground.

"I would never," he says, "hire someone who tells me that they really just want to work for humanity. I want to know that they'll love the work they're doing, and be good at it." Grossman himself made sure that he would be good at the work by designing his own apprenticeship in nonprofit organization management for several years before accepting the position at Outward Bound.

Sometimes, you can't follow your heart. Career counselor Phyllis Edelin of Philadelphia had a client who was let go from a well-paid executive position with AT&T in the Chicago suburbs. Because he had managed his finances well, he was in a position to pursue his dream job: working at a hardware store answering people's questions about hardware. He loved the job, but his wife simply couldn't adjust to his new identity, because so much of her self-image was wrapped up in his being a prestigious executive. He ended up quitting and getting a "real job."

So, in the jungle of our fantasy, you might decide to search for some ultimate goal, some heroic mission there, that would be a burning driving force in your life.

Richard N. Bolles, *The Three Boxes of Life, and How to Get Out of Them*

Mike Cambridge, president of Cambridge Staffing in Cedar Rapids, Iowa, says the biggest mistake most people make either in job interviewing or in job performance is not understanding the chemistry of personalities. "People who get fired most [often]," he says, "are either highly dominant people who are great at turnarounds, but tend to have difficulty in steady or compliant organizations, or highly compliant people who tend to be politically naive."

False humility can be even more harmful than false pride, because it causes you to set limits too low on what you're capable of achieving—in your own mind and in the minds of others.

Follow your heart but watch your step. Joy Baker's life revolved around horses, which led her to veterinary school. After six years of working in research, however, she was becoming frustrated by the growing pressures to raise grant money. At the same time, she was increasingly busy giving riding lessons to young people who had been left hanging when a local teacher quit.

Joy felt a calling to get back to horses and to kids—her two loves—but also knew it would be a business with high risk, and for which obtaining necessary financing would be difficult. She spent six months working on a business plan before finally quitting her job and starting the business. In short order, she needed to build a new barn with an indoor arena to accommodate growth. She was able to get additional financing from the bank because her original business plan had been so persuasive, and because she had made all of her target projections during the first year of operation.

If you want to know your own mind, there's only one way: to observe and recognize everything about it.

Thich Nhat Hanh, *The Miracle of Mindfulness*

Mark Ziniel worked construction all the way through college, then got a job as a manager with Cargill. He hated it. Although he had to work long hours, he felt that most of the time he spent was useless activity. He finally quit and went back to work building things.

"I get immediate feedback from my customers and can see the results of my work," he says, adding that he often hears highly paid professionals say they wish they could be doing his job instead of theirs.

Create art. You may not see yourself as being creative or artistic. Most of us have these talents squashed flat under the steamroller of the three Rs. Reinflate it. For a guidebook, read *The Artist's Way: A Spiritual Path to Higher Creativity* by Julia Cameron. The principles, tools and exercises will help you remove blocks to your creativity. They'll also help you confront your own fears of being creative. Cameron wrote the book after she quit drinking, which she had previously used as a catalyst and a crutch for her creativity.

"The idea that I could be sane, sober and creative terrified me," she said, "implying, as it did, the possibility of personal accountability. 'You mean, if I have these gifts, I'm supposed to use them?' Yes."

Here's another shibboleth about creativity that you must let go—the notion of "art for art's sake." In her book *The Reenchantment of Art,* Suzy Gablik says that art must be more than art. It can and should have a purpose. Self-transformation, she says, cannot come from ever-higher material expectations; "it's more likely to come from some new sense of service to the whole—from a new intensity and personal commitment."

Be truthful with yourself in answering this question: Would you be happier living in a glorious big house paid for by your toil at a boring job you hate, or living in a small cottage spending your workdays creating something that is beautiful in your eyes because of its purposefulness in service to others?

People who recognize their potential are constantly bridging the gap between inner and outer. They invest the external world with meaning because they disown neither the world's objectivity nor their own subjectivity.

Anthony Storr, *Solitude: A Return to the Self*

Bill Needler, a career consultant in Milwaukee, says mid-career people who lose jobs frequently take positions that don't suit their skills, or invest in businesses that they aren't temperamentally equipped to manage, because of their anxiety about generating cash quickly. Financial desperation, he says, can be the insidious cause of financial failure. Rather than rushing into something that's not right for you, try slamming the brakes on your spending to give yourself time to figure out what's right.

Don't daydream. Create memories of the future. The subconscious mind cannot distinguish between reality and imagination, and will work to create the reality of the images you set before it. The more precise, intense and tangible you can make these memories of the future, and the more frequently and vividly you replay them in your mind's eye, the more likely you are to create them in your reality.

Quantify the money you're making for your organization. If it's less than your salary, spiff up your resume.

True story: Two high school classmates went their own way after graduation, and both eventually became doctors. One traveled the world, climbed mountains, doctored people in exotic places and lived his life as an adventure. The second became a respected specialist, settled down and raised a family. At a reunion, the first person complained of having nothing to show for his experience. The second complained of having much to show at the expense of having missed experience. Follow your dreams, but know that there's always a price.

Thinking about your values helps in your search to find purpose and meaning in your life and work. Setting priorities requires you to think more deeply about what is important in your life. Through identifying and evaluating your values, you can get to know yourself better. With every decision you make, no matter how small or large, you are making a statement about what matters to you.

David P. Helfand, *Career Change*

Allow yourself to give any meaning you choose to your nocturnal dreams, then believe in the results. For example, if you dream of a huge, odoriferous landfill, you might interpret it as the burying of your anger, fear, low self-esteem or other malignant emotions. If a phone rings during one of your dreams, of course, it's the call to offer you the job of your dreams.

Harvey Mackay suggests in the book *Sharkproof* going to an industrial psychologist and completing personality tests on your own. Go to a firm with an excellent reputation, he recommends, which can give you a sound and objective interpretation. There are two benefits: first, you'll learn something about yourself; second, knowing about yourself and being able to show the initiative for having tested yourself will help differentiate you from other candidates in the job market.

When Bobbe L. Sommer, Ph.D., decided she wanted to become a professional speaker, she fell back on the old adage, "Fake it till you make it." She visualized herself as a speaker, joined the National Speakers Association, and began making cold calls to potential clients. She built her goals around the SMART formula:

*S*pecific goals.

*M*easurable goals.

*A*ction plan.

*R*ealistic.

*T*imely.

Monika Freidal, a vice president in Milwaukee for outplacement firm Lee Hecht Harrison Inc., describes a case where introspection and flexibility saved a job. A top executive with a major telecommunications company was about to be terminated because she couldn't get along with her boss, he being a micro-manager and she being very independent. She sulked for a while and contemplated leaving the company. Finally, she made a complete inventory of her skills, which she took to the vice president for human resources. He was so impressed that he became her ally and helped her find a more appropriate position within the company.

Most career decisions today involve some trade-offs in terms of your work values or the skills you want to use or your areas of interest; you seldom get everything you hope for met in a career. You'll likely have to make compromises because of reality—both yours and the job market's.

Linda Peterson, *Starting Out, Starting Over:*
Finding the Work's That's Waiting for You

A comprehensible description and explanation of the various personality and aptitude testing devices is contained in the book *Career Change* by Dr. David P. Helfand. In Chapter 5, Helfand describes the Strong Interest Inventory (SII), which shows how similar your interests are to others, and the Myers-Briggs Type Indicator (MBTI), which shows your personality preferences and how they compare with others.

"One potential problem with the SII and MBTI," Helfand says, "is that they can be easily misinterpreted. Sometimes they aren't interpreted at all; some counselors merely hand their clients the results. Not only is this a detriment to the client, but it's also unethical career counseling as well."

In the book *Zen and the Art of Making a Living*, Laurence Boldt describes the paradox of profound professional change. The more significant the change you are making, the more you need the support of others. The bigger the change is, however, the less likely others are to understand and support what you're doing.

Sometimes, you just have to hang in there on your own until things start working.

You should try your hand at reducing your principles to writing, or, at the very least, writing down principles that appeal to you and fit your circumstances, even though they may have been articulated by others. If not in open view, your principles should be kept in your mind's eye for both guidance and inspiration.

William J. Byron, *Finding Work without Losing Heart*

If you're in a job-search support group, Martin Asdorian, managing director and president of LAMA Associates, emphasizes that it should be occupationally focused. The support group should have three primary functions: First, all members should try to help each other; second, each should present detailed information on any job leads uncovered, excluding those they're actively pursuing themselves and might have competition from someone else in the group; and third, gossip. Asdorian suggests that a support group might need a facilitator, so that administrative work doesn't interfere with anyone's job search.

If you're asked to take personality or aptitude tests, consider that it may be for your own good. According to Ken Voges of Red Bud Industries, a machinery manufacturer in Illinois, these tests have helped improve the company's retention. Perhaps surprisingly, Voges says that people with a high mechanical aptitude but whose attitude would make them a poor fit with the company culture invariably do poorly, whereas people with a good attitude tend to do well, even with a lower mechanical aptitude.

Recall the convoy principle that was used to escort shipping across the Atlantic during World War II in order to fend off

Nazi submarines: The slowest ship determines the speed of the whole. In the same way, the weakest link in your own matrix of skills is probably the determining factor in how successful you can be in your career. Find those key weaknesses and work on them.

A great difference between winners and losers is their attitude towards what they need to know. Losers feel it's someone else's job to teach them everything they need to know. Winners are determined to learn, and will seek out the best possible training, if necessary, completely on their own.

John Lawhon, *Retail Selling*

Don't try to get rid of bad habits—replace them with good habits. For example, if you've a habit of making snap judgments about people or events, try to replace it with the habit of not creating opinions about anything for at least two days so that your intuition has time to mull things over.

One of the most complete and comprehensive self-help books you can buy is *Og Mandino's University of Success*. This book includes excerpts from 50 of the greatest self-help classics of all time.

Discipline is developed doing small things, many of which you'd rather not do, perfectly; then you keep on doing them until they become habits. Then you do a little larger thing, perhaps slightly more difficult or tedious or unpleasant, perfectly; then you keep on doing it until it becomes a habit. Then you do something more difficult, or more of the same thing, and continue until you've built up your tolerance.

Steven M. Finkel, *Break Through: How to Explode the Production of Experienced Consultants*

See if your library, local college career planning office or nearby high school has DISCOVER, the computerized career-planning system from American College Testing (ACT). The Guidance-Plus Information part of the system will ask you to complete inventories of your interests, abilities, experiences and views. If you've completed them, it will also incorporate your scores from the Myers-Briggs personality profile and the Strong Interest Inventory. Then, based on the resulting profiles, it will suggest a number of possible occupations by reporting your inventory profiles on the system's "World-of-Work Map." The system also includes templates for completing resumes and cover letters, tips for lead research and interviewing and information on virtually every post-secondary education institution in the country.

The Career Design computer software program from Crystal-Barkley Corp. in New York includes a series of self-discovery and planning exercises. It can take 40 or more hours to complete, and walks you through three basic questions: Who am I? What do I want? How do I get there? The software may be available at your local computer store at a cost of just under $100, or can be ordered by calling 800-346-8007.

Make a list of teachers and mentors in your life, and the most important things you've learned from each.

Not using aptitudes you are blessed with tends to cause a lot of frustrations, and can inhibit career success.

Stephen Greene, Johnson O'Connor Research Foundation

When you read motivational or self-help books, listen to tapes or attend seminars, don't let them make you feel inadequate. Motivational speakers and writers seem to have their act completely together, and may seem not to understand why you don't. Just remind yourself that you can't be all things to all people, but you can continuously and incrementally raise your standards and improve your performance. Who knows, maybe someday you'll be up there on the stage!

Turn your greatest weakness into a strength. Many great speakers became great by making a commitment to overcome their shyness in public. Many great motivators struggled to overcome low self-esteem.

Take the advice of samurai warrior Takeda Shingen: "If only a man will not do what he himself would like to do, and do those things that he finds unpleasant, his position, no matter what it is, will be much improved."

When things do not turn out [as we had expected], we feel like failures. We will never be happy until we stop measuring our real-life achievements against that Dream. We will never be comfortable with who we are until we realize that who we are is special enough.

Harold Kushner, *When All You Ever Wanted Isn't Enough*

Read the poem "If" by Rudyard Kipling. Trust in yourself, dream and think, and give it your all: the earth and everything in it will be yours.

I f you participated in high school or college athletics, at one point or another a coach probably told you that you only cheat yourself by loafing during practice. The same is true in your career. Taking the easy way out, temporarily trading off job security for loss of true work fulfillment, working to less than your true potential, and giving in to emotional negativity or physical lethargy are only cheating yourself (and perhaps your family).

Much evidence testifies that people who are emotionally adept—who know and manage their own feelings well, and who read and deal effectively with other people's feelings—are at an advantage in any domain of life, whether romance and intimate relationships or picking up the unspoken rules that govern success in organizational politics.

Dan Goleman, *Emotional Intelligence*

I n 1990, James Heuerman, a vice president and senior partner for Korn/Ferry International, a San Francisco executive recruiting firm, went to Mexico by himself for six weeks. The experience helped him evaluate what he'd been doing for the previous 25 years. Upon his return, he got rid of many of the activities and trappings of his earlier career, and realigned his priorities to provide more time for family and personal life. Early in his career, he says, he was motivated by a fear of failure, and not wanting to let other people down. Now, however, he's finding that by lightening up on himself, he's motivated by more positive emotions.

P repare yourself for a lifetime of learning and change. David Lutz, Director of College Level Assessment and Survey Services for ACT, says that "people who graduate from college today will find that their knowledge may be obsolete within five years." He points to the nursing profession, where five years ago the half-life of a college training program was seven and one-half years; today it's five years, and in five years it will likely be less than three years. In order to avoid career obsolescence, Lutz says, you must keep reading, think critically, communicate well and continue to develop your quantitative and analytical skills.

We are moving toward a new freedom in the workplace where each human spirit can create and expand, not because our spirit—or theirs—is being controlled but because it's unlimited. Only then can we truly tap the human spirit and watch it take flight.

Terri R. Hoyland, *Tapping the Human Spirit*

"Quite frankly, gentlemen, I don't think you appreciate the gravity of this situation!"

2

Managing Your Thoughts and Emotions

If you're looking for a new job, you'll likely be competing against other candidates with comparable experiences and accomplishments. In most cases, the offer will go to the person who seems to be the best fit with the organization's chemistry. If you're happily employed, your ability to reign in your emotions and respond appropriately to events will be as important to your long-term success as your technical skills and knowledge—perhaps even more so.

Self-confidence is the trait of envisioning victory from situations where others see only defeat, to find promise where others find grounds for pessimism, to see opportunity where others see obstacles.

James B. Arkebauer, *Ultrapreneuring: Taking a Venture from Start-Up to Harvest in Three Years or Less*

You cannot manage the world, and you cannot change the people around you. The only things over which you have immediate control are your own thoughts and emotions. Spend time every day to understand the reason you think and feel the way you do, and consciously mold your thoughts and emotions in a positive direction.

Winston Churchill once said that we first shape our buildings, then our buildings shape us. How much more so with our thoughts and emotions. Pay attention to your thinking, your moods and your attitudes, because they are inexorably making you into the person that you are to become. You aren't your thoughts, emotions and attitudes—to become the person you want to be, figure out the ways you need to think and feel in order to be a success, then consciously manage your mental processes to think and feel just that way.

As far as I'm concerned, people who think they fear failure have got it wrong. They really fear success. If you truly feared failure, you'd be very successful. *People who truly fear anything stay as far away from it as possible.*

Barbara Sher, *I Could Do Anything if I Only Knew What It Was*

According to Thomas Dolan, president of the American College of Healthcare Executives, of the more than 1,000 executives served by the College's outplacement service, not one lost a job as a result of technical incompetence. More than 90 percent of the success of a health care executive, he believes, will be related to interpersonal skills. And effective interpersonal skills require effective management of your thoughts and emotions.

In a 1995 survey of top executives by Accountemps, it was found that 90 percent said a good sense of humor is important for anyone hoping to reach senior management. Here's how one top hospital executive used humor to help him cope with career crash: The day after he was fired, he was out doing his son's paper route. A former colleague drove by, saw the man trudging along with the newspaper bag over his shoulder, then quickly drove off as though he had seen a resurrected leper. Imagining how the story of his precipitous fall from corner office to street corner would grow in the telling cheered the ex-big cheese immensely.

A fear of commitment is perhaps the most deadly of all, because it's not simply your failure to commit to a plan of action—more importantly it's a failure to commit to yourself, your hopes, and your dreams. Underlying a lack of commitment is low self-esteem. To be successful, you have to believe that you deserve success. You have to have an image of yourself so tangible that you can reach out and touch it.

Peller Marion, *Crisis-Proof Your Career*

The Course in Miracles states that the opposite of love is not hate, it's fear. Faith is the underpinning of the courage required to conquer fear. Take several evenings to read through the Bible looking for inspirations of courage.

As I wrote in my book *Never Fear, Never Quit: A Story of Courage and Perseverance,* caring is the root of courage. If you care enough about something, you'll find the necessary courage. On the other hand, laziness—not fear—is the root of cowardice. It takes moral energy to confront your fears bravely. To live an effective life, you must first and foremost conquer your own laziness.

Understand the ways that your conscious mind can distort reality:

Over-generalization: "Bad things always happen to me."

Labeling: "I'm a chicken."

All-or-nothing thinking: "If I don't get this job, I'll just die."

Selective filtering of facts: "The good performance appraisal and pay raise mean nothing; the boss didn't smile this morning, so I'm sure I'm on the hit list."

Invidious comparisons: "I'll bet Jack Welch wouldn't have any trouble getting this job done."

Inappropriate role reactions: "It's budget day—I think I'll curl up in bed and call in sick."

Jumping to conclusions: "Did you see all the suits going into the board room? The big layoff must be coming!"

Blowing things out of proportion: "This is the second time I've been fired. I'll be branded a failure for life."

Denial and minimization: "Well, I didn't get the report done on time, but it's no big deal; they never read the things anyway."

Personalizing: "I knew that my department would take the biggest cuts, because the boss never did like me."

Just as fire transforms the energy of a dead tree into warmth, light, and protection, so our fears ignite us. They create energy that can prepare us for danger before it arrives, stimulate us to take action, and keep us moving when we are exhausted.

Art Mortell, *The Courage to Fai*

A void these killer attitudes:

Hopelessness: The three greatest attributes, said St. Paul, are Hope, Faith and Love. It's hard to imagine a person having faith or feeling love if they themselves are devoid of hope.

Learned helplessness: No matter what it is that you think you can't do, someone else has already done it with even fewer resources and greater obstacles.

Pessimism: Expect the worst and you'll usually get it.

Cynicism: Look for higher motives in other people, and expect goodwill and good faith. Life's too short to live waiting for a knife in the back.

Worry: A vast majority of the things people worry about never happen. Chronic worry is an incredible energy drain.

Boredom: The greatest existential fear of human beings is the possibility that life has no meaning. Boredom is the primary symptom of a meaningless life. If you're bored, get busy!

Seeking blame: John Wooden, coach of the powerful UCLA basketball dynasty, said that failure begins when you start to blame others for your problems. Take charge and take responsibility for your life, problems and all.

Plan for the worst, expect the best and understand the difference between positive thinking and wishful thinking. Positive thinking is working for something and expecting it to happen; wishful thinking is waiting for something and hoping it will happen.

[This is] one of the central paradoxes of evolution: the adaptive skills of the past, which have made it possible for us to exist in the first place, do not necessarily make life easier or happier now.

Mihaly Csikszentmihalyi, *The Evolving Self:*
A Psychology for the Third Millennium

Whenever you find it tough to believe in yourself, make a list of other people who believe in you. Try to put yourself in their shoes and make a list of the reasons why they think that you've got something important to offer in this world.

Life is a battle between exhibition and inhibition. We all want to shine, to learn new things, to become the best at what we do, to be recognized for our unique assets and contributions—to exhibit our best. Yet we also all confront powerful inhibitions, forces that would keep us invisible and inactive. To the extent anyone leads a rich and fulfilling life, and makes significant contributions to his or her profession, it's because the exhibitionary forces have overwhelmed the inhibitionary forces.

To change your circumstances, first start thinking differently. Do not passively accept unsatisfactory circumstances, but form a picture in your mind of circumstances as they should be . . . believe and succeed.

Norman Vincent Peale, *The Power of Positive Thinking*

"Attitude is everything." That realization led Jeff Keller to leave the practice of law and start a business to help motivate others to live life with a positive attitude. He is a frequent speaker, publishes a newsletter and sells products adorned with his company logo: "Attitude Is Everything." For more information call 800-790-5333.

The most dangerous time for middle-aged men is 9 A.M. on Monday; there are more heart attack deaths at that time than any other. Create a Monday morning ritual for yourself that helps you prepare yourself emotionally for the coming week. Give yourself the gift of early morning solitude to get yourself spiritually centered, emotionally calm, and to envision yourself having a highly energetic, productive and cheerful week. The time you invest may save your life.

Here are two pearls of wisdom from that ancient Chinese book of wisdom, the *I Ching:* (1) Every negative thought must be purged before it takes root; (2) Forgetting the ego is the highest form of rest.

*It's quite possible that you'll get over your depression more
quickly if you recognize it to be a spiritual crisis, which very
often it is . . . . It's only through such suffering and crisis that we
grow.*

M. Scott Peck, *Further Along the Road Less Traveled*

Here's another admonition from the *I Ching* that can help you
get ahead in your career: By relentlessly examining your own
motivations, and watching the impact that your words and actions
have on others, you can transcend egoistic bias, have a clear perception of reality and do what is right for all concerned.

In his book *Managing,* Harold Geneen, the former CEO of ITT
Corp., stated that egoism was a more destructive disease in corporations than even alcoholism. Here's a paradox: the praise, success and material gain that gratifies your ego can stultify growth
of your soul, and as a result put an artificial limit on your ultimate
career potential.

*Doubt is torture. If we give ourselves fully to something, it will be
clearer when it might be appropriate to quit. It's a constant test
of perseverance.*

Natalie Goldberg, *Writing Down the Bones:
Freeing the Writer Within*

After having been fired for the second time in as many years,
one hospital administrator conducted an in-depth analysis of
behavioral patterns that had contributed to his failures. He was intense but fragmented; impulsive and impetuous; cared deeply but
was inconsistently effective; was opinionated and judgmental; and

better at starting things than finishing them. Seeking professional help, he was diagnosed with adult attention deficit disorder. Through a combination of professional counseling, better organizing his work and daily meditation, he has learned to observe and question impulsive thoughts and emotions before acting upon them, and to question his first impression of external reality in stressful situations.

Here are some of the ways that we allow unwarranted fear to keep us from becoming the people we are meant to be:

Doubt and indecision: "I'm going to quit this hateful job. Well, maybe tomorrow—if it looks like I'm going to get fired anyway. Unless . . . Oh, I just don't know!"

Worst-case thinking: "They'll replace me with a machine; I'll never find another job; the kids will have to support us by working at McDonalds."

Arbitrary deadlines: "I must have a new job by the end of the year."

Unrealistic quotas: "I'm going to make 100 cold calls today."

Procrastination: "I said I'd have it done by today? Uh-oh."

Ignorance: "How come nobody told me I'd have to pay taxes on unemployment compensation?"

Avoidance thinking: "Well, at least all this downsizing won't affect my job, since what I do is so important to the company."

Sometimes we've done all the preparation we could for something; there's nothing else we can do—but we still sit around in fear. This is the point when you must use the antidote *to fear: you must make a decision to* have faith, *knowing you've done all you can to prepare for whatever you're fearing, and that most fears in life rarely come to fruition.*

Anthony Robbins, *Awaken the Giant Within*

Fear of success is far more dangerous than fear of failure, because the subconscious mind works to prevent that which it fears. People may fear success because of low self-esteem and a feeling of not deserving it; because it will increase the hassle factor in their lives; it will increase what others expect of them; or it will run them headlong into the Peter Principle. Fear of success shows up as anxiety, acceptance of mediocrity, lack of focus and concentration, not working well under pressure and not keeping promises. Here are some steps to overcome fear of success:

1. Clearly define your purpose and goals.

2. Why did you choose those goals? Why do you deserve to achieve them?

3. What is the service component; how will other people benefit from your success?

4. Study role models who have accomplished similar successes before.

5. Pray for help in achieving and coping with success, acknowledging that it's acceptable to pray for your own success as long as it's with the understanding that a higher will be done.

6. Every day, visualize yourself in your new successful role; make it as tangible as possible—a "memory of the future."

7. Do the thing you most fear to do, and do it now.

Fear of success is sometimes manifested as a sort of internal circuit breaker. If it seems like things are going too well or too fast, and you suddenly run out of steam, ask yourself whether fear of success has pulled the plug on you, and if so, go plug it back in.

That's one of the peculiar things about bad moods—we often fool ourselves and create misery by telling ourselves things that

simply are not true. *And the strange thing is that we usually don't have the vaguest suspicion that we're being conned by our misery and self-doubt.*

David D. Burns, *The Feeling Good Handbook*

If you smoke, quit. It will help you in your career, since almost all hiring managers will hire a nonsmoker over an equally qualified smoker. Moreover, there's a strong relationship between smoking and being depressed. This may be as a result of the physiological action of the drug nicotine in the brain, and the oxygen-suppressing effect of carbon monoxide in the blood. Or, it may just be your soul weeping at the sight of you slowly committing suicide.

Staying on top of your time and your money will work wonders for helping you stay on top of your thoughts and emotions. For a crash course on the most effective time and money management system ever devised, order the special report, *No Brainer Time and Money Management* from Paradox 21 Press (800-644-3889).

Anger spurts a cloud of darkness, rendering people visionless, unable to see the reality of their lives. Fear and anger, always together, you never have one without the other.

Jack Hawley, *Reawakening the Spirit in Work*

There seem to be two schools of thought on the subject of depression. People who approach it from a religious or spiritual foundation see it as a message from the soul that some deep personal need must be attended to before you can make further progress on your path in life. Those who approach it from a peak performance perspective see in depression an avoidable hindrance to the depressed individual, optimizing their contributions to self and society, and even as a form of laziness that inhibits one from getting to the important work at hand. If you're depressed, ask yourself who's speaking? Is it your soul trying to tell you that you're on the wrong path and that fundamental change is necessary? Or is it your ego complaining about how hard and unfair life is? If it's the former, better shut up and listen. If it's the latter, get off your can and get to work.

You've probably heard the title of Susan Jeffers' book *Feel the Fear and Do It Anyway*. For many people, laziness is as big a barrier as fear. We often misinterpret mental or emotional fatigue with physical fatigue and do exactly the wrong thing—like taking a nap when the most rejuvenating action would be getting a project done that has been hanging over our head. Try this surefire formula for success: *Feel the fatigue and do it anyway.*

If we learn to accept our imperfections with humor, as the reflection of our very humanity, we will experience humility and tolerance, we will understand that we are already filled with forgiveness, we will see the gift of our lives, the chains will fall away, and we will be free—free not so much from fear or "dependence," but free for love, for life itself.

Ernest Kurtz and Katherine Ketcham, *The Spirituality of Imperfection Storytelling and the Journey to Wholeness*

Study the iron law of cause and effect. All things happen for a reason, because something has made them happen. If you are in the job market, you'll get hired because you put together and implemented a job search plan, not because the stars had destined you to be out of work for just so long before becoming reemployed. All the world's motivational speakers will tell you: "If it's to be, it's up to me."

Here are two surefire ways of getting a better handle on your thoughts and emotions: keeping a daily journal, and daily meditation. A daily journal can be as simple as a spiral notebook in which you record your thoughts and emotions at the end of each day, or it can be an extensive exercise in self-evaluation, like the one included in *The Self-Transformation Workbook* (800-644-3889). Meditation can help you understand and let go of thinking or emotional patterns that are self-sabotaging in nature.

Your worst enemy cannot harm you as much as your own thoughts, unguarded.

Buddha

Don't confuse verbs and adjectives with nouns. Losing a job (verb) or being a losing candidate (adjective) does not make you a loser (noun).

Take a dozen of the negative labels that you apply to yourself and convert them into realistic descriptions. For example, "I'm lazy" might become, "I find it hard to get motivated to do work for which I don't see a real benefit."

Placebo yourself: The Placebo Effect refers to the phenomenon of sugar pills making people well simply because they believe they're taking medicine. Identify some food, activity or location that does something positive for you, like increasing your energy or bringing you a sense of peace. Then allow yourself to believe that every time you expose yourself to that "placebo," it will have the desired effect.

One of the central troubles that human beings fear is the waste of their potential. Again and again the sadness that people long to share with their friends or counselors is a sense that we're going nowhere.

John Carmody, *How to Handle Trouble: A Guide to Peace of Mind*

Hawthorne yourself. The Hawthorne Effect refers to the fact that people are more productive when they think they're being observed. Every week, make some small change in your environment that you believe will make you happier or more productive. Imagine that someone you really want to please is watching to see how the change will enhance your productivity. The more strongly you believe that the effect will occur, the more likely it is to do so.

Buy some subliminal music tapes and listen to them when you're driving, reading, or relaxing. Believe that they'll have the desired effect and it's likely that they will. Some of my favorites are "Enhancing Success" and "Self-Esteem" by Steven Halpern, "Abundance" by Stuart Wilde, and the four subliminal tapes that come with the Anthony Robbins tape program Personal Power.

Forget the self and you'll fear nothing.

Carlos Castaneda, *The Art of Dreaming*

Here's a personal productivity system that's fun! Create a mental cartoon task force and empower each of its members to take charge of a certain phase of your life, to push you ahead when you feel like sitting it out. Here are some suggested task force members:

▶ A bean counter, complete with green eyeshades and a Bob Cratchet quill, to give a cold eye to every expenditure, and make you sit down with your checkbook at least once a week to balance your finances.

▶ A Marine drill instructor to give you some old-fashioned high-decibel motivation when you can't drag your tail out of bed on those cold mornings, or can't bring yourself to do those unpleasant jobs like cleaning out the garage or making a networking call.

▶ A university professor who can take charge when you have important material to review or new subjects to learn. You may find that the professor has a hard time keeping the Marine drill instructor out of the picture for very long, since there's no end to unpleasant jobs that need to be done when you're trying to study, so give your professor a strong backbone.

▶ A Zen master full of wisdom and peace to help you always keep your attention in the here and now.

▶ A circus clown to keep reminding you that all work and no play will make you dull, listless, and a bore to be around.

In his book *Full Catastrophe Living,* Jon Kabat-Zinn says that a regular practice of meditation is one of the most effective ways to manage stress in your life. His follow-up book *No Matter Where You Go, There You Are* includes many effective meditative exercises.

Self-criticism increases our fear and belief that living a blemish-free existence is necessary. The only cure is to help ourselves feel secure within ourselves, so that we eventually come to see that no matter what we do, we will not cast ourselves out of our own hearts.

Marsha Sinetar, *Do What You Love, the Money Will Follow*

Meditation can be an effective source of stress management, but don't expect it to bring instant bliss or enlightenment to your life. A disciplined practice of meditation is hard work, and can create great emotional pain as you work through and let go of the pettiness of ego. As Charlotte Joko Beck said in her book *Everyday Zen,* "The truth is, we like our drama very much. People tell me they want to be free of their troubles; but when we stew in our own juices, we can maintain ourselves as the artificial center of the universe. We love our drama. We like to agonize and complain and moan." Unfortunately, she concludes, our dramas often end in tragedy, and we are better off letting them go.

Try reverse wink meditation. Sit quietly with your eyes closed. Then, every five minutes or so, quickly open and then reclose them. Spend the intervening five minutes concentrating on a complete mental re-creation of what you saw. Let any other thoughts or distractions flow through as you rivet your thoughts on the mental picture of the space in which you are sitting.

Regular meditation not only restores our inner harmony and vital energy, but provides us with an actual experience of the peace we seek.

Diane Dreher, *The Tao of Inner Peace*

In his classic *The Book of Five Rings,* the great samurai swordsman Miyamoto Musashi stated that true wisdom begins when one transcends a petty preoccupation with one's own thoughts and emotions, and begins to see the world from a transcending and objective perspective. Miyamoto won every fight because he had long since given up the need to win.

In their book *The Warrior's Edge,* military special forces experts John R. Alexander, Richard Groller and Janet Morris recommend "cross crawls" to stimulate both hemispheres of the brain. The simplest cross crawl exercise is marching in place with the left arm and right leg lifting in unison, followed by the right arm and left leg. This should be done in a free-flowing, relaxed, and stress-free manner. Ten minutes or so every day will enhance energy and creativity.

Courage gives consolation, patience, and experience, and becomes indistinguishable from faith and hope.

Paul Tillich, *The Courage to Be*

In his book *Advanced Selling Strategies,* Brian Tracy says that most people earn at their "self-concept level of income." If you want to increase your earnings, he says, "you must increase the amount you believe yourself capable of earning. You must raise your aspirations, set higher goals, and make detailed plans to achieve them." Fear of rejection, more than anything else, holds people back from achieving their full potential, and fear of rejection is often based on low self-esteem. The best way to improve your self-concept, and enhance your self-esteem, is through "systematic desensitization," continuously doing what you are afraid of doing, and trying to do it better every time.

Respond to whining and negative inner voices with positive and constructive affirmations. Like these:

Self: I am God's child, made with Love and blessed by Grace. I will find the inner strength and courage to deal with whatever life brings me, because God is with me.

Relationships: I build strong relationships because I genuinely care for other people. Because I try to be a good friend, I have many friends who support me when I am down.

Work: I invest energy and enthusiasm into making my work a work of art that is an expression of my inner spirit. I love my work, and feel called to doing it to the best of my ability.

Possessions: I work hard to earn the possessions I have and wish to have, and am generous in sharing my wealth with others.

Faith: I believe that things happen for a reason, that part of the challenge of human life is to learn the lessons of adversity, and that I have no need for worry but only to work and pray in good faith and what is meant to be will be.

In a notebook, list the many choices that are available to you that can change presently upsetting experiences into positive ones . . . . In every situation there are at least 30 ways to change your point of view.

Susan Jeffers, *Feel the Fear and Do It Anyway*

In the early part of this century, the great psychologist and philosopher William James said, "The emotions aren't always immediately subject to reason, but they are always immediately subject to action." Make your every action positive and upbeat, and your emotions will follow.

Time is life. How much of your life are you killing every week with thought-deadening and emotion-dulling television?

Never put anyone or anything down, including yourself. Suspend judgment. People tend to find what they're looking for. Look for the best in others and in yourself. You'll find it.

Effectiveness in daily living can be further enhanced by the practice of meditation in action, which means maintaining an awareness of the breath while performing everyday activities.

John Harvey, *The Big Book of Relaxation*

Sometimes it's more important to forget the old than it is to learn the new. Assume that you've been hypnotized; many of your self-limiting beliefs are simply not valid in fact. For example, if you believe that you just can't do math, take a math course at the local community college and prove to yourself that with diligent study you *can* learn the material.

If the pressures of work make it difficult for you to manage your thoughts and emotions, consider the following comments from several great athletic coaches: Tommy Lasorda of the Los Angeles Dodgers says, "'Pressure' is a word that is misused in our vocabulary. When you start thinking of pressure, it's because you've started thinking of failure." Sparky Anderson of the Detroit Tigers says, "Those who worry about getting fired know in their heart that they can't do the job. I never worried about keeping by job. Those that get fired are the ones that can't deal with it. Call me and fire me. I'll find a job tomorrow. That's the only attitude you can have."

He who has conquered doubt and fear has conquered failure. His every thought is allied with power, and all difficulties are bravely met and wisely overcome . . . . Thought allied fearlessly to purpose becomes creative force.

James Allen, *As a Man Thinketh*

Adopt the "no Xs" philosophy of life: no excuses, no exceptions, no extensions.

Next time you find yourself swamped in self-pity, pick up the books, *Chicken Soup for the Soul (first, second and third*

helpings) by Mark Victor Hanson and Jack Canfield. Just a few pages and you'll find renewed hope, optimism, and vigor.

To be courageous . . . requires no exceptional qualities, no magic formula, no special combination of time, place and circumstance. It's an opportunity that sooner or later is presented to us all.

John F. Kennedy, *Profiles in Courage*

Just because your phone's not ringing doesn't mean no one loves you. Use the opportunity of solitude to improve your mind and your attitudes.

Consider whether it's possible to positively manage your emotions in the context of your organization's environment. Arthur C. Martinez, CEO of Sears, Roebuck & Co., told *Business Week* that "Part of my job is to keep a vague sense of unease percolating through the entire company." While your boss might think that a vague dread is necessary for the success of the organization, you may want to consider whether it's worth the personal price you pay for living with it.

There's time and hope if we combine patience with courage.

Winston Churchill

"We're not very big on salary increases, but the size of your office will expand annually."

3

Managing Your Space

Frederick Taylor, who brought industrial engineering to our economy in the early part of the twentieth century, left a bitter legacy in some regards. But in at least one way, he was right on target. The better you organize your space to minimize wasted motion—including the time you waste looking for lost items—the more productive you're able to become.

Your space says a lot about who you are, and it may say things to others that you would just as soon they not perceive. Being from "the other side of the tracks," living in "the boondocks," having space that looks like "the city dump" can all label you in the eyes of others. More important, your space will inexorably begin to influence your self image. Think carefully about the spaces in which you choose to live and work, and put love and pride into them.

A telephone should never be more than an arm's reach from where you intend to sit and do the bulk of your job search work.

Max Messmer, *Job Hunting for Dummies*

Before diving into the question of how your workspace is configured, raise the question of where it's located. Are you spending unnecessary time on a commute when you could more efficiently be working from home? Could you be more effective relocating your office to be closer to key suppliers or customers? Are you operating out of one office when two would be more efficient, or vice versa?

In his book *Managing with Power,* Stanford professor Jeffrey Pfeffer emphasized the importance of being centrally located in the communications grid for anyone aspiring to a position of power and influence. Both in terms of your physical space and your spot in cyberspace, think about how you can position yourself centrally in the communications network. Many futurists believe that the high-tech edge of our society will create a high-touch backlash, so don't neglect to be strategic about your physical space, thinking that you'll never have to see anyone except over the Internet.

Frederick Taylor and industrial efficiency have gotten a bad rap in recent years because too many managers have used the principles to simply "speed up the assembly line." But by organizing your activities so as to minimize wasted motion, you'll get more work done in less time. Try this: go to a handful of fast-food restaurants during the next two weeks and observe their operations carefully. Which are the most efficient? From each location, get at least one idea for how you can increase the efficiency of your own workspace.

If you have an office away from home as well as a work area at home, try to take best features of each and apply them to the other.

In his book, *The Reinvention of Work,* Matthew Fox describes work as part of the sacred creative process by which we become fully human. Put loving care into the design and configuration of your workplace; make it your own sacred spot for creativity. Establish mini-rituals for your workspace—for example, never enter it without stopping for a quick deep breath to clear your mind and mentally focus on the next key priority.

Put one thing of exquisite beauty or special meaning in your workspace, and train your mind to see that thing as a cue to stay in the present. Imagine your workplace as having walls that keep out regrets of yesterday and fears of tomorrow.

If possible, designate separate sections of your workspace for different tasks. For example, my office is located in what used to be a two-bedroom apartment. One bedroom is furnished with cushions, low tables and a standing desk; this room is for meditation and creative writing. The other bedroom is furnished with a conventional desk and is used for business, research and editorial writing. The former living room contains library, warehouse and business office functions. When my body enters a given space, my brain is already beginning to get into the right mind-set.

Order a catalog from Successories (800-535-2773). You have probably seen their ads on airplanes and seen their products in the offices you visit. You can get pictures of beautiful settings with motivating sayings for your walls, neat stuff for your desk and books for your mind. I recently purchased real rocks carved with inspiring quotations for each of my children, and am pleased to report that they are placed prominently where they do their homework.

If you have space for a small pinboard or whiteboard, these can be used to write down your goals, reminders, affirmations and even a bit of humor.

Put some thought into color, even if you're limited to small accents. Try this: have a spot where you can affix a small piece of ribbon, and have different colors to help you attain the proper state of mind for each task. Put up a red ribbon when you need to race through a long list of phone calls; a blue ribbon for something requiring deep thought; a yellow ribbon when you need to remind yourself to be patient.

As long as it's assigned to you, truly make it your space. Whenever you are there, don't let your mind be somewhere else. Invite people in for a brief visit. When you run out of steam, do push-ups or meditate. Don't just sit there; take frequent walks around the boundaries of your space.

The nineties are a time of great creativity in office design and furnishing as businesses seek to use space more productively. It's also a time when you can have fun designing your office to reflect your personality and work requirements.

Kathleen R. Allen and Peter H. Engel,
Office Design That Really Works!

Experiment with your space layout. If you have an office, move the furniture around. If you are in a cubicle, reorganize your work surface. Pay attention to what works and what doesn't, and commit yourself to a process of continuous improvement in your space management.

In their book *Office Design That Really Works,* Kathleen R. Allen and Peter H. Engel say that the image you create in your office is important because an organized workplace enhances morale, builds respect and trust, saves time and energy and fosters ownership. Even if you are running a job search from your home, take pride in your work area; act as though it were your own little business office, which it is. You'll find yourself feeling more capable and professional than if you are working in a disorganized mess.

Ideally, you should design your area with two separate work surfaces. On the first will be your personal computer, telephone, fax machine, printer, rolodex and supporting supplies and references. The second should be relatively clear, and used for planning, writing and other work. An L- or U-shaped desk works well for this purpose.

In an article on office furniture, *The Wall Street Journal* reporter John Pierson found that extended sitting is responsible for much of the lower back pain that eventually strikes 90 percent of us. To prevent this from happening to you, first get a chair that is ergonomically designed to support your back. Second, move around frequently, and try working standing up whenever possible (for example, when you're on the phone).

Use trays or baskets to organize your desktop. This might include in, out, and pending, with a separate file folder for reading. The pending file is not for long-term storage, but rather for items to be done by day's end, pending further research or activity. Anything that remains undone at day's end should be put into your suspense file for the day that you plan to deal with it. Your desk should also be close to references that are frequently used (telephone books, directories, dictionary, and so on) and key supplies (stapler, sticky notes, tape, writing utensils, stamps, and so on). Anything that you use more than once a day (say, thank you cards) should be close at hand.

Time management experts uniformly agree that your workspace should not be papered with sticky notes. Get into the discipline of keeping your reminders on one master list or in your daily planner. Don't decorate the walls with scraps of paper.

Take this tip from Ann McGee-Cooper from her book *Time Management for Unmanageable People;* go to your nearest full-service office supply store and browse. Don't get carried away, but if you see products that can help you be more organized, give them a try.

Put a perpetual motion machine (available at most gift shops) on your desk as a continuous reminder that time keeps moving and you should, too.

Here are 10 space-saving behaviors you can adopt to keep your workspace as efficient as possible:

1. *Be decisive.* Never put a piece of paper in your pending file because you don't know what to do with it.

2. Return calls promptly so that pink slips don't pile up.

3. Rather than typing response letters, scribble a note at the bottom and return the incoming letter. Don't keep a copy.

4. When you read a document, summarize key points and keep only the summary, rather than highlighting and keeping the entire document.

5. Trust your filing system so that everything doesn't have to be on your desk.

6. Trust your daily planner so that everything doesn't have to be on your desk.

7. Create a map of your desk and your workspace and then keep everything in its assigned place.

8. Get a bigger recycling bin and garbage can and empty them more frequently.

9. Don't pile up things you don't need.

10. Computerize.

According to a study published in *The Wall Street Journal,* the average office worker spends six weeks every year looking for lost papers and other items. Organize all your files into four basic file types: tickler files, working files, reference files and archival files. The tickler file should include folders numbered 1–31 and January–December, and should be checked each day.

Working files contain materials regularly needed for current active projects, and should be in a desk drawer or close to the desk. Reference files include references not routinely needed, but which should be reasonable accessible (for instances, recent articles on strategic planning). Archival files are papers that will probably never be accessed again, but for legal, sentimental or other reasons must be kept. These can be bundled away and stored off-site.

Einstein was right—space and time are relative: make your space more efficient, and you'll have more time to focus your energy on what really needs to be done. Managing your space gets your attention on the true task at hand.

Mary S. Murphy, MSM Effectiveness Coaching

In her book *Organized to Be the Best!* Susan Silver suggests five main steps for organizing files:

1. Categorize all existing files as either active or inactive, and remove inactive files from the existing file system.

2. Write out all categories and subcategories of filed information on paper, involving everyone who will be using the system.

3. Physically set up the system, having on hand an adequate number of folders, labels and other necessary supplies.

4. Create a master file index or chart and label all drawers, and if appropriate, introduce the system at a staff meeting.

5. Maintain the system by sticking to a solid filing routine.

Throw away junk mail as it comes in; don't even open it.

When any newspaper or magazine comes in, throw away the old one after reading the table of contents and briefly scanning through it and tearing out any articles of lasting interest. If you're not willing to be that ruthless, then take the old issues home over the weekend, and if they aren't read by Sunday evening, recycle them or throw them away.

Organize your briefcase. Have a standard set of supplies that you might need while on the road (such as pens and pencils, notepads, airtight plastic bags, paper clips, small stapler, transparent tape, sticky notes and so on). Get a briefcase big enough to hold two 8½ × 11 documents side by side so that you can readily carry your daily planner, documents from work or the job search, a small laptop computer, a few newspapers and magazines and a good book.

Efficiency expert Stephanie Culp emphasizes the importance of being organized whenever you go for an interview. If you have to dig through a purse or briefcase for a pen or a resume, she says, you're only going to annoy the interviewer. Streamline your "luggage" and make sure that anything you might need is close at hand.

If you go for a job interview, think about the strategic presentation made by your open briefcase. A student's backpack stuffed with papers is obviously a one-way ticket home. But a nice, well-organized briefcase that, when opened, reveals a state-of-the-art laptop computer, *The Wall Street Journal* and a business journal or two and the latest book on business (ideally the one that's been making the rounds of the company where you're interviewing) can make a great impression. It won't be hard for you to find an excuse to open it up for the interviewer to see.

Be prepared wherever you go. Author Robert Fulghum wears a multipocketed vest in which he keeps pens and paper, a small dictation unit and a larger pad so that he can write wherever the inspiration strikes him.

Organize your car for maximum productivity. Rubbermaid makes a number of great products that can help you turn your car into an office on the road. If you're well organized, you can turn commuting downtime into productive uptime (and wouldn't you rather be spending your downtime doing something other than looking at the bumper in front of you?).

If you're in the job search mode, organize your workspace for optimum efficiency. Here's a great way to do it and have fun at the same time: call it your Job Search War Room. Put maps up on the wall with stickpins marking the location of target companies. Place all of your target company files in milk crate-style file boxes so that they are readily accessible. Build your command and control center around the computer and the phone. Once a day, bring in your spouse or friends for a briefing. Pretend. Before long, you'll be having more fun and a greater sense of effective urgency.

If you're in outplacement, you may be given space at the outplacement firm or in a career center. Although you'll (hopefully!) only be there a short time, apply all of the same principles to your space. Make it cheerful and efficient; decorate it with the things that lift your spirits; play your music softly. If it's a space that you share with others, pack your things efficiently so that it's easy to set up shop every day you go in.

Attend to the rituals regarding other people's space. When you enter someone else's space, do so with respect. Pay attention to how the space is organized and to the tools being used to see if there are good ideas you can take back to your space.

Know which spaces to stay away from. Avoid the "water cooler" where people gather to grumble about how awful everything is, both because you don't want to be seen with a negative crowd and because their cynicism may rub off on you. Avoid the smoking area, because smoking is increasingly being seen as something that a person of intelligence and judgment would have quit long ago—it's a career-limiting addiction. Besides, you don't want anyone to smell your clothing and assume that you're a smoker.

If you're starting a new business, you'll need to consider both efficiency and presentation in your decisions about space. For example, it may be more efficient and cheaper for you to work out of home, but your potential customer base may expect you to have a more prestigious address. This is especially true if you're in a field like advertising, where image is so important. Some people have finessed this by working from home, but leasing a mailbox with a prestige address or arranging for space sharing.

Don't neglect the most important space of all—that which lies between your ears. Get into the discipline of regularly retreating into your inner space, especially during times of doubt and worry, to seek the clarity of your original vision and mission. Make sure that your inner space is not cluttered by negative emotions and groundless fears. Make it a welcoming respite into which you can retreat when seated on a full airplane next to a crying baby.

Space we can recover, time never.

Napoleon Bonaparte

"Whatever you do, don't let them talk you into accepting time off in exchange for overtime pay."

4

Managing Your Time

Time is the one true equal opportunity employer; we're all blessed with the same 24-hour day. Yet virtually all successful people share one characteristic: they're extremely conscious of using their time effectively, and rely on organized systems to help them do so. There are many different systems on the market to help you organize projects and manage time more effectively, ranging from simple paper-and-pencil calendars and to-do lists to sophisticated computer systems. What type of system you use is less important than your willingness to discipline yourself to use one.

We often try to cram in so many activities that we don't give ourselves enough time to enjoy any of them.

Jeffrey J. Mayer

In the well-known children's story, the velveteen rabbit was obsessed with becoming "real." When do we become "real" as people? What is it that makes us real? It's our work. The work we put into forming our habits and character; the work we put into building relationships; the work we put into serving others; the work we put into making the world a better place for ourselves, our families and humanity. Are you real? Make a list of all the things you did in the last month at your job. How much time did you spend on real work—meaningful work that makes a difference in the world? And how much did you spend on busy work, pretend work and make work that creates nothing and leaves no legacy? Do you need to wake up, change your priorities and get real?

In Thomas Cleary's translation of *The Book of Leadership and Strategy: Lessons of the Chinese Masters,* one reads that, "The affairs of sages are limited and easy to manage. Their requirements are few and easy to satisfy." Be ruthless with your time, concentrating it on those things that matter, and you'll be amazed at your productivity. And there you have the secret formula for *No-Brainer Time Management:* just say no to tempting distractions.

Jesus was a man who got things done, yet he always seemed to have time for people. In her book, *Jesus CEO: Using Ancient Wisdom for Visionary Leadership,* Laurie Beth Jones describes some of the ways that Jesus made time. One of the most important was that he guarded his energy. He did not waste physical or emotional energy on judging others, negative self-talk, argumentation or procrastination. Over the ages, many people have tried to emulate Jesus in order to be better people; Jones shows how you can emulate Him in order to be a better time manager.

Understand how your self-image and self-esteem influence your time-management skills. People with low self-esteem often waste lots of time agonizing over whether they even deserve the favorable outcomes that would come with getting something done. Indeed, low self-esteem can be a sneaky disguise for laziness ("I don't deserve a job like that, so I won't even apply"). If you feel stuck, spend some time every day creating a visual mental image of yourself as a winner, a caring and deserving person whose success will help not only yourself but the many others you care for.

I use my head by asking myself a practical question, and I con-
sult my heart by asking myself a private question. Then, after I
listen to myself and others, I make a better decision and act on it.

Spencer Johnson, M.D., *"Yes" or "No":*
The Guide to Better Decisions

Many of us feel guilty for "doing nothing," for just sitting and thinking, or just sitting. But it's often when you just sit and think that the important questions arise, and it's when you just sit that the answers to those questions come to you.

Be patient. Rainer Maria Rilke wrote in his *Sonnets to Orpheus:*

In spite of the farmer's work and worry,
He can't reach down to where the seed is slowly
transmuted into summer. The earth bestows.

Motivational speaker and author Anthony Robbins says that most people overestimate what they can accomplish in one year, but dramatically underestimate what they can get done in ten years. Be patient—even Superman spent most of his time as Clark Kent.

Give yourself measurable goals. More important, measure your progress toward completing them. For example, if your goal is to make 100 networking calls in a week, each day summarize your progress so that you don't find yourself with 89 calls to make on Friday afternoon, just as the people you want to reach are getting ready to go to the country for the weekend.

Brian Tracy is a highly successful author and speaker specializing in development of the human potential and personal effectiveness. His story illustrates the up-front time commitment, sacrifice and patience required to achieve excellence. As he told *Sharing Ideas* magazine:

> In my first three years, I had to liquidate all of my savings, sell my house, borrow from my friends and relatives, and move into rented premises with my young family in order to continue giving seminars. Gradually, like a plane in a nosedive, I managed to pull up, level off, and begin to climb . . . . I was in my seventh year of full-time speaking before I began to really be successful.

Here's a paradox: many workaholics aren't very effective time managers, despite their long hours, and ultimately end up burned out. Ann McGee-Cooper's book *Time Management for Unmanageable People* lists ten questions you can ask yourself to see if you're slipping into workaholism, which can cause you to devote all of your time to urgent but not important activities. These questions are:

1. Does your personal identity substantially derive from your work?

2. Do you challenge yourself to work more than everyone else?

3. Do you take pride in being more productive than everyone else?

4. Do you frequently take work home?

5. Do you take work on vacations or other recreational activities?

6. Do you drag work home and not get to it because you're too exhausted?

7. Do you deny yourself having fun because you're afraid you won't get back to work?

8. Do you think wistfully about all of the things you'd love to do but could never find the time because of all of your work?

9. Do you feel anxious if a weekend goes by with nothing accomplished.

10. Are you critical of others who spend large blocks of time with "nothing to show for it?"

McGee-Cooper says if you answered yes to most of these questions, you may be a candidate for burnout.

One of the disciplines of building a rich soul life seems to be the simple act, on a daily basis, of remembering what is most important to us.

David Whyte, *The Heart Aroused: Poetry and the Preservation of the Soul in Corporate America*

In researching for this book, I reviewed more than two dozen books on time management. They all contain valuable information and recommendations, and there's not one that contains everything. If I were forced, however, to recommend a single time-management book, it would be *Time Management for Dummies* by Jeffrey J. Mayer. Mayer is one of the nation's leading time-management and personal effectiveness consultants and author of multiple books on the subject. What makes this book stand out is its impressive scope. It's not limited to how to be more efficient in your work, but also contains rich advice on how to be more effective in your work.

In his book *The Seven Habits of Highly Effective People*, Stephen Covey says that, "The challenge is not to manage time, but to manage ourselves." He believes that the problem that most people have is not inadequate discipline, rather that they've not deeply internalized their priorities. First, he says, know who you are and what your goals are; and then develop your discipline, which he defines as, "the ability to make and keep promises and honor commitments," by achieving small "private victories."

Here are ten potential small personal victories you can strive for:

1. Write down your goals, post them where they can be seen, and review them every day.

2. Each night plan for the next day; each noon take a few minutes to check your progress and plan the afternoon.

3. Get up half an hour earlier than usual for exercise and meditation.

4. Gradually begin to replace watching TV with reading good books.

5. Make every nonessential phone call 50 percent shorter.

6. Walk 50 percent faster.

7. Catch up on your work so well that you can quit at noon on Friday.

8. Every hour ask yourself if the activity upon which you're spending your time is the most important for achieving your key goals.

9. Build mini-sabbaticals into your day—five minute interludes for prayer and reflection.

10. Every day, blast your way right through at least one mental block that is urging you to slow down and take it easy.

Think about your habits and routines. A habit is a behavior that becomes second nature and is done without conscious thought; a routine is a method or sequence of organizing work to make it more efficient and consistent. Make a list of bad habits that you'd like to break (for example, spending time watching television in the evening) and good habits you'd like to cultivate (reading a good book in the evening). Make a list of new routines that could help you be more productive (for example, tackling your most important and difficult project first thing every morning) and current routines that could be changed (making calls and responding to mail as the urge strikes rather than at a designated point of the day).

There are many systems available on the market (for example, Franklin Daily Planner, Day Runner, Time Design, and others) and you should use one or develop your own. In his book *The 13 Secrets of Power Performance,* Roger Dawson describes a simple yet elegant system that can be put into any three-ring binder. The important thing is to make sure that it fits your needs and to keep it simple.

Being an artist means: not numbering and counting, but ripening like a tree, which doesn't force its sap, and stands confidently in the storms of spring, not afraid that afterwards summer may not come. It does come. But it comes only to those who are patient, who are there as if eternity lay before them, so unconcernedly silent and vast. I learn it every day of my life, learn it with pain I am grateful for: patience *is everything!*

Rainier Maria Rilkie: *Letters to a Young Poet*

David D. Burns, M.D. says in *The Feeling Good Handbook* that we must recognize the many positives to procrastination: it's easy; we can do more enjoyable and relaxing things; we can, for a while, forget our problems and avoid hard work; we can frustrate the people who are nagging us; and we can prevent people from pressuring us to do more work by proving our unreliability. Stop pampering yourself and take responsibility for becoming the person you want to be and for doing the things you want to do. And do it now.

Think about what happens to someone who has promised to do something for you, and they keep putting it off. Pretty soon, they feel guilty. They start to avoid you. Your appearance reminds them that they have unfinished work to do, and they start to resent you. You, meanwhile, are wondering how to get the promise fulfilled without resorting to unpleasant behavior. Before long, a friendly relationship can become strained and may even break. Whenever you find yourself putting something off, consider the real long-term costs, which may include loss of friends and tarnishing your reputation.

G ood things come to people who wait, but they're the things left behind by the people who hustle. Are you working for things to happen or waiting for things to happen? If your job search center is more waiting room than workspace, stoke up your sense of urgency.

K enneth Blanchard, co-author of *The One-Minute Manager,* suggests that every day you complete at least one task that will bring you closer to the completion of your goals. That way, you'll avoid the natural tendency to put things off to the last minute.

P rocrastination is the root of much evil and can be a cause of frustration in one's career, personal finances and personal happiness. Robert Grudin, in his book *Time and the Art of Living,* notes that procrastination is robbing the future for present comfort. Delaying a needed action, he says, is simultaneously admitting its necessity and refusing to do it. Habitual procrastination is disrespect for the future, and paradoxically forces the procrastinator to live in the past, facing yesterday's undone chores.

T he most important principle for overcoming procrastination is to not wait until you feel inspired, but to go to work right now. As Robert H. Schuller said in his book *Tough Times Never Last, but Tough People Do:* "Use your head and your heart will follow. Don't wait until you feel like it to make the move. If you wait until you feel like it, emotion will run you instead of reason."

Kerry Gleeson founded a company that provides time management training internationally. He hammers away on the theme that Do It Now is the most important principle of success. Gleeson feels so strongly about the Do It Now approach that he says that it almost doesn't matter whether or not you're doing the right thing, so long as you're doing something; if you know what you want and are action-oriented, you'll eventually succeed.

In his book, *The Personal Efficiency Program: How to Get Organized to Do More Work in Less Time,* Gleeson described having worked with one executive on the Do It Now philosophy. When he came back for a follow-up visit, the executive remarked that it was the most effective tool he'd ever used. Yet Gleeson noticed a pile of papers in the pending basket. He picked up a phone slip and said "Why don't we call him now?" "Now?" the man asked, clearly more comfortable with putting it off. Do It Now must become a regular, daily practice—one that Gleeson believes is the secret to being effective at work and at life.

For us, living simply meant reducing the scale, maintaining the comfort, eliminating the complexity, and minimizing the time demands of life as we had known it in the 1980s.

Elaine St. James, *Simplify Your Life: 100 Ways to Slow Down and Enjoy the Things That Really Matter*

Bob Young, northern regional manager for Time Design, says that when people say they are disorganized it usually means they don't know where to start. He provides the following guidelines for prioritizing all those things you need to do:

1. Write down everything you must, should or would like to do. This exercise will take some time as the list should be exhaustive.

2. Make distinctions between major projects, interim tasks and things you would like to do if only you had the time.

3. After you've identified your major projects, establish the next immediate action for each project.

4. All next-step actions will fall into one of only two categories: it must be done today or it will never get done; everything else.

5. Do what must be done today, and then evaluate the everything else list and do those tasks that are essential to your long-term vision.

When setting your priorities, ask co-workers, family members and friends what they think your priorities should be. You may be surprised by what you hear.

In his book, *How to Get Control of Your Time and Your Life,* Alan Lakein suggests coupling two principles to create an effective philosophy of time-management: Assigning all tasks a priority code of A, B or C; and The 80/20 rule, by which is meant that 80 percent of the value of your time comes from only 20 percent of the items on your list. Most of us carry the "C" items on our list week after week, feeling guilty about them. Here are two alternatives: Drop them off the list and forget about them forever; or give yourself a big chunk of time (maybe a long weekend) to get your "C" file cleaned out so that you can concentrate on top priorities with renewed energy.

One reason for procrastination is becoming paralyzed with all of the possible negative outcomes of taking action. As Rafe stated in my book *Never Fear, Never Quit: A Story of Courage and Perseverance,* "Fear is many tomorrows, but courage is one today." Don't worry about all the possible futures over which you have no control; concentrate on the one today that is within your power to influence.

Combine the advice of AA and Nike:

One Day at a Time.

Just Do It.

Many people are incapacitated with depression and/or panic attacks. A common reason for these emotional lows is an overhang of uncompleted work. Once the work is done, you'll wonder—with a sigh of relief—why you even dreaded it. If you're depressed, try simply getting to work on the most unpleasant task facing you right now, and forget about the cruel world that seems to be crushing you down.

A glance at your weekly calendar may reveal how much of your time is eaten up by the pursuit of success and how little is left over for personal growth. Have meetings become habitual rather than essential? Once-productive routines merely spinning the wheels? What can you drop? What would you like to add?

John R. O'Neil, *The Paradox of Success*

Read all of the time management books, and you'll come up with a mechanical prescription for overcoming procrastination that reads pretty much as follows:

1. Make a list of all the reasons why you want to or need to accomplish the particular task.

2. Make a list of all the factors that are blocking you from doing it.

3. Sketch out a plan for breaking down the task into manageable chunks and for accomplishing each chunk.

4. Be patient and be positive; keep reminding yourself why you're doing it, and praise yourself for your progress.

5. Give yourself big blocks of time for each chunk, to minimize gearing up and downtime.

6. Be decisive ask yourself what is the worst that could happen, and if that is acceptable, proceed forthwith.

7. Stick with your decisiveness: plow right through doubts and second thoughts.

8. Change gears the minute you sense yourself bogging down.

9. Reward yourself for each completed chunk, and reward yourself lavishly for completing the project.

If you're not into mechanical solutions to the procrastination problem, here's one that will delight your right brain. Create a small imaginary army of cartoon characters, each of which are assigned to tackle a specific part of the procrastination problem:

▶ A little gardener with pruning shears, clipping away all of the "shoulds" that may be keeping you from focusing on the most important job at hand.

▶ A big roadworker with a jackhammer blasting through all of the resistance keeping you from what you want to be doing.

▶ A demolition squad that will take all of your negative thoughts and emotions and bulldoze them into a big pile and blow it to smithereens.

▶ A crew coming out with big cans of industrial strength glue with which to affix your butt to the chair until the job is done.

▶ A clown running around with balloons to keep everybody's spirits up through the drudgery.

▶ A scorekeeper standing up on an old-fashioned scoreboard keeping you posted of the inning and the score.

One great way to overcome procrastination is to find joy in the work itself, irrespective of the outcome. Why is it, the Zen master would ask, that you like sitting in a jacuzzi and dislike having your hands in warm dishwater?

If you really need help with time management, consider taking a course. Here are several possibilities:

▶ American Management Association's two-day course on basic planning techniques ($1,085 for nonmembers; 800-262-9699).

▶ Covey Leadership Center's First Things First course ($295; 800-331-7716).

▶ Franklin Quest's one-day TimeQuest seminars ($195; 800-983-1776).

▶ Time Design ($325, including complete management system, or $175 if you already have a Time Design system; 800-742-7257).

▶ Time Power by Boardroom Inc. ($175; 800-625-2424).

If an item remains on my list of less important items for a couple of months, I declare it dead and have a brief moment of silence to honor its passing. Then I throw it out with whatever appendages are tied to it, such as guilt and remorse.

Anne McGee-Cooper, *Time Managemen*
for Unmanageable People

Most people not only procrastinate daily activities, but procrastinate really living. Here are three books that can help you find what it is you would really love to do for a living:

▶ *Stop Postponing the Rest of Your Life* by Paul Stevens.

▶ *I Could Do Anything if I Only Knew What It Was* by Barbara Sher.

▶ *Love Your Work and Success Will Follow* by Arlene Hirsch.

Proverbs 20:13 says: "Do not love sleep or you'll go poor, stay awake and you'll have food to spare." Mike Walden of Detroit, Michigan, is one of the greatest cycling coaches in the world. He suggests the following wake-up routine each day before breakfast:

1. Scrub your entire body to get the blood flow going.

2. Jog in place for two minutes.

3. Do several minutes of static stretches including trunk twist, toe touches, arm stretches and neck rolls.

4. Do three sets (10 each) of push-ups and abdominal crunches.

5. Do five deep-breathing exercises where you inhale as deeply as possible, then totally empty your lungs.

Getting into the discipline of doing this every day will help you wake up and be more alert so that you can make better use of your time.

Have a pile of routine "busy work" somewhere in your office to work on during mental down times, when your brain isn't up to doing more demanding things.

Keep a good book and a few current business magazines in your briefcase so you can keep up on your reading when you're being kept waiting.

When you're traveling, take a supply of envelopes and stationery so that you can complete thank you notes, fill out travel expense reimbursement forms and take care of routine correspondence so that it's not sitting in a pile on your desk when you get back home.

As a professional stand-up comedienne, Jane Condon of Greenwich, Connecticut, knows the value of timing, including recognizing the benefits of not being discovered prematurely. "My acting teacher keeps telling me to just do the work and enjoy the journey, and that when I'm ready I'll be discovered." The *I Ching* advises that one should best mature undisturbed, and not let ambition outstrip ability to deliver. In her eight years as a comedienne, Condon has entertained the President, been reviewed in *The New York Times* and *The Wall Street Journal,* and had other recognition, but still she is in no hurry for fame and fortune. Her favorite headline is from a small newspaper that reported, "Comedian Lives Normal Life."

Time management can help you have fun. Simon W. Ulmer, a vice president with Schuller International in Denver, sets an example by dedicating one hour during the middle of each day to exercise. He does so because it's important to him, but also because it encourages associates to balance their lives.

Eric Harvey and Alexander Lucia, in their book *144 Ways to Walk the Talk,* suggest taking a vacation in your office. Get your boss and colleagues to agree to leave you alone for a while so you can get your desk cleared off and catch up on overdue promises.

The essence of time management is to set priorities and then to organize and execute around them.

Stephen R. Covey, *Principle-Centered Leadership*

Mary S. Murphy is principal of MSM Effectiveness Coaching in the Philadelphia area, providing one-on-one coaching for executives who are feeling overwhelmed and out of control at work, and generally in their lives. She begins with a philosophical approach. The client first needs to accept that they are responsible for their own "mess," and that clarification will come through their efforts. Second, they need to forgive themselves for any negative self-judgment they may have made as a result of their old habits. This acceptance and forgiveness will help provide the mental clarity required to manage their new systems and workflow more effectively.

If difficulty paying attention, impulsiveness or a tendency to jump from one thing to another keeps you in a state of perpetual disorganization, consider the possibility that you may have the symptoms of adult attention deficit disorder. According to Dr. Thomas Spencer, assistant director of pediatric psychopharmacology at Massachusetts General Hospital, "This is a real condition in adults." The condition can be treated by imposing a more disciplined organizational structure upon yourself, and in some cases by medication such as Ritalin. In Dr. Spencer's studies, 80 percent of patients studied improved with Ritalin, compared to only 4 percent in a control group. If you think this might be causing you difficulty, consider seeing a physician.

Burt Holtje, editor of *Agency Sales* in Laguna Hills, California, suggests solving the problem of unreturned phone calls by leaving a compelling reason why someone should call you back. This is, of course, a creative challenge to someone in job search mode. Something like, "I could add a million dollars to your company's bottom line," is probably more compelling than, "Please call me at this number."

To minimize phone tag, on your answering machine, suggest that anyone leaving a message also leave the best time for you to return the call.

Writer's block is often caused by inadequate research; the same can be true in the job search. If you don't know what to say in a cover letter, or aren't sure what to include in your resume, chances are you don't know enough about the company you're targeting. Rather than wasting your time trying to write your way through a block, put down the pen and either hit the books or hit the road to do more research.

If you're out of work and think there's no one to whom you can delegate, think more creatively. Much of the manuscript for the book that is in your hands right now was typed by my 14-year-old daughter, who in a number of cases also provided editorial improvements. As an added benefit, we got to spend some time together, and she's learning more about the business world.

Put a time management system on your computer. Read the book *ACT! for Dummies* by Jeffrey J. Mayer for a good description of how to use one of the best-selling products.

Pick a musical selection that you associate with mental vitality, and whenever your energy begins to flag, put it on. Some possibilities from the classical repertoire include: either the first movement of Beethoven's 5th Symphony or the last movement of his 9th; Dvorak's 9th Symphony, "From the New World"; Wagner's The Ride of the Valkyries; the Sabre Dance from Khatchaturian's ballet Gayaneh; Tchaihovsky's 1812 overture; or Borodin's Polovtsian Dances.

The basic concept behind using a Master List is that by writing everything down in an orderly, meticulous way, you can do a better job of staying on top of all your unfinished work, tasks, projects, and correspondences. When you put things down on paper, you don't have to remember as many things.

Jeffrey J. Mayer, Time Management for Dummies

Envision your life as a daily drama, an episode in the eternal epic struggle for survival. As Carlos Castaneda said in describing the teachings of Don Juan, the man of knowledge must respond to circumstances with dramatic exertion. He says:

> The idea of impending death created not only the drama needed for overall emphasis, but also the conviction that every action involved a struggle for survival, the conviction that annihilation would result if ones exertion did not meet the requirements of being efficacious.

Read the book *Ziglar on Selling* by Zig Ziglar, and especially the chapter "Organization and Discipline." Ziglar states that while many people think disciplined organization will restrict spontaneity, in fact the opposite is true. Developing a successful sales tracking (or job search) system is essential to being an effective person. Ziglar suggests that about 70 percent of all sales are made between 7 A.M. and 1 P.M.; try to reach people early when they are energetic, optimistic and responsive. To make it big, make it early and follow the following tips:

1. Make your time count by selling in "downtime" with administrative activities, maximize the time you have for real (revenue-producing) work.

2. Be willing to work that extra hour and you'll see terrific results.

3. Get some help so that you can delegate nonrevenue-producing tasks. Ziglar cites a study showing that 47 percent of the top producers at Re/Max Realtors have personal assistants.

4. Analyze your time using a time log to keep track of your activities. Ziglar said that little more than two hours a day are typically spent in actual revenue-producing activity.

5. Keep careful records of your results. (Ziglar says that failure to do so is, "A lazy, stubborn, closed-minded, loser's response.")

William S. Frank's book *The Job Search Time Manager* is a 90-day calendar and note-keeping system that you can use to keep your work organized and to retain important notes pertaining to your job search. It also includes inspirational quotes and humorous cartoons.

Subscribe to Soundview Executive Book Summaries (5 Main Street, Bristol, Vermont 05443). Each month you'll receive a package with two or three eight-page book summaries that are three-hole punched for easy storage, as well as several shorter reviews. If you've not been keeping up on the business literature, you might want to invest in back issues as a way of boning up for interviews.

If you're a manager, one of your most important responsibilities is keeping yourself and others focused on work that produces actual results. In the book *No Excuses Management,* T.J. Rodgers, chairman of Cypress Semiconductor (with William Taylor and Rick Foreman) says:

> Most people want to achieve. And most people are capable of extraordinary levels of commitment and performance—much

more than their bosses give them credit for. Yet all too often organizations have trouble distinguishing between "real work"—things that make a difference in corporate success—and the "drone work" that gets done because it's always been done or because some boss arbitrarily decides that it should be done. People know when what they're doing doesn't matter—and it leaves them demoralized and demotivated.

Live your dreams before they come true, just in case you never wake up.

McZen, *The Sound of One Hand Working*

S queeze some time out of your conversations. Remember Shakespeare's advice: Brevity is the soul of wit.

T hink of the last time you went on vacation and how much you got done the day before. Fool yourself into thinking that every day is the day before vacation. You'll get a lot more done, and you'll live your life with a sense of excited expectation.

T here are times when your time isn't really your time, but belongs, or should belong, to someone else. You want to sleep, but your sick child is crying for attention; you want to read a novel, but the roof is leaking; you want to attend a power lunch at the country club, but morale is low at the plant. Here's a paradox: when you stop seeing your time as something that belongs to you, you'll approach the task at hand with a more positive mental attitude and probably complete it much sooner, earning back some of the time that was not yours to begin with.

We've all been advised by time-management experts to spend two weeks keeping a detailed log of how we spend our time. Most of us think this would be unnecessary, and believe that we've an intuitive grasp anyway. But when Peter Drucker asked a group of corporate CEOs to tell him how they spent their time and then studied how they actually were spending their time, he found almost no correlation between the perception and the reality. For the next two weeks, keep track of every 15-minute increment of time, what you did and what was accomplished. If nothing else, the Hawthorne Effect will probably cause you to have an incredibly productive two weeks.

Let your subconscious mind work for you while you're asleep. Just before you drift off, plant a perplexing question, and when you wake up, immediately write down all of your dreams. You may be surprised at what you discover. When Elias Howe was stumped in his work to invent a sewing machine, he had a dream in which soldiers carried spears with holes at the end, giving him the idea for the needle that broke his mental bottleneck.

Make use of your subconscious mind to work on important problems while you're conscious mind is working on merely urgent ones. Nikola Tesla could design a piece of machinery in his mind, set it running, and periodically come back to it in coming months and see where it was wearing down. You may not be the engineering genius that Tesla was, but chances are your subconscious mind is churning away, wearing out other things—like an unpleasant colleague, an unforgiven slight, a fear of poverty or other such things. Challenge your subconscious mind with the tough questions you face in your life and give it deadlines by which to report back to you. You'll be amazed at what you learn, if you listen receptively.

Most experts in networking will tell you to make good use of breakfast, lunch and dinner for networking opportunities. Think twice, however, before scheduling a meal when a telephone call would suffice. Not only will you save lots of time, you'll be picking up fewer restaurant checks.

Procrastination is a habit. Break that habit first, then worry about prioritization. Many people use prioritization as an excuse for procrastination.

Kerry Gleeson, Founder, Institute for Business Technology

Don't ruminate after rejection. It's tempting, after a lost sale or job rejection or other setback, to spend time in self-pity. It's much more productive, however, to use the rejection as a stimulus to redouble your efforts and move on ahead.

The most powerful four words in the English language may well be: "If it kills me." When you set out to do something important, promise yourself that you're going to finish the job even "if it kills me." You'll find that not only does it not kill you, it does—as Nietzsche promised it would—make you stronger.

Improve your memory. Take a course, listen to a tape series or buy a book. Much time is wasted looking up forgotten information, patching up things we forgot to fix and relearning lessons. It's possible through training and disciplined effort to improve your memory, and this can be an important element in your efforts to manage your time.

"We've got to stop meeting like this!" How many times have we all thought that, yet we go on meeting like this. An excellent guide for making the most of meetings is the book *Meetings: Do's, Don'ts and Donuts* by Sharon M. Lippincott. Following is a brief list of ground rules developed by one corporate team for their meetings:

▶ Arrive and start on time.

▶ Be there.

▶ Be prepared.

▶ Share responsibility for following and enforcing the ground rules.

▶ Stick to the agenda.

▶ Listen respectfully and thoughtfully.

▶ No interruptions, side conversations, phone calls or other disruptions.

▶ No silent observers.

▶ No "killer phrases" like "we tried that before."

▶ Have fun with appropriate humor.

▶ Use consensus to make major decisions.

▶ Be realistic when accepting responsibility for follow-up tasks.

Be aware of the time culture of the organization for which you work or for which you're applying. Some organizations put a high premium at working effectively to maximize people's free time, while others expect that you'll be there late into the evenings and on Saturdays whether you have real work to do or not. It goes without saying that you'll be much happier working at an organization that fits with your personality than trying to change your personality to fit your organization.

Get enough sleep; if you're chronically tired, you'll waste time by being inefficient.

Don't wait for the phone to ring, and don't agonize when it doesn't. You can't control when or if other people will call you, but you can increase the odds that it will happen by keeping a steady stream of calls and letters going out of your office.

Basho, who elevated the poetic form of Haiku to a high art, said that "A poet must discipline himself every day." Self-renewal and self-improvement is a daily struggle. Every day remind yourself of your purpose in life. Every hour remind yourself to focus on key goals.

You cannot have fun at work if you don't deliver results. But no matter what your results, if you're not having fun and leading a balanced life, you won't live up to your ultimate potential as an individual or an organization.

Simon W. Ulmer, Vice President and General Manager for
Business Development, Schuller International of Denver

Early in this century, the noted American philosopher/psychologist William James commented that most people are capable of accomplishing much more than they think, if they would simply work through their fatigue. They will, he said, almost always gain a second wind of energy. Try it for a month; every time you feel so fatigued that you have to lie down for a nap or park your backside in front of the boob tube, force yourself to keep working for another fifteen minutes and see if the good Dr. James wasn't right.

Buy a three-minute egg timer—the kind with sand in it, like a mini-hourglass. Keep it by the phone and watch the minutes slip by as you converse. Make it your goal to limit every call to one flip of the timer, with important calls getting two flips. This excludes, of course, calls where you're seeking detailed information or speaking with someone who is in a position to substantially affect your future career.

Buy a one-hour timer with a bell, and use it to give yourself deadlines. Say, for example, you've been dreading that much-needed rewrite of your resume. Lay out everything you'll need and set the timer for one hour. Then work like crazy to get the whole job—right down to the last typed period on the page—done before the timer goes off. If one hour is unrealistic, give yourself two dings. Make a game of it—a game you take as seriously as Joe Montana took football.

Get in shape. What's this got to do with time management? Plenty. It's a paradox that the stronger your body is, the more it will bend to your conscious commands, but the weaker it is, the more it will dictate what you may or may not do. Becoming physically stronger will give you the stamina to persevere when you'd rather quit, and to focus your energy more intensely so that you can squeeze a minute's worth of work into each minute spent at the desk.

If you don't want to program your activities too tightly because you're afraid it will inhibit your ability to be spontaneous, consider the words of Frank Bettger, a professional baseball player who went on to become one of the nation's most successful salesmen and wrote the book, *How I Raised Myself from Failure to Success in Selling:* "I prefer to work on a tight schedule four and a half days a week and get somewhere than be working all the time and never get anywhere."

Here are five things that can help you be more productive on your telephone:

1. Use a headset, freeing up both hands for writing or typing on your computer. I use one made by Plantronics (800-426-5858).

2. Have two telephone lines, with the second being an unpublished rollover number. Connect the first number to your answering machine, and always use the second line for outgoing calls, to minimize the times you need to put someone on hold to answer the phone.

3. Use a long cord, or better yet a radio phone to give you mobility while you talk.

4. Hook up your phone to your computer and ACT! or other contact manager system so that it can dial the phone for you.

5. Sure, they're expensive, but get a portable phone. The time you save in returning calls during downtimes will more than make up for the cost.

If you're working from home, make your home office every bit as professional as it would be in a high-rise tower. In their book *Successful Telephone Selling in the '90s,* Martin D. Shafiroff and Robert L. Shook tell of a successful Beverly Hills real estate agent who makes her most important networking calls from home in the morning. Although she could get away with it in her bathrobe and curlers, before she picks up the phone, she carefully puts on makeup and a crisp business suit. It helps her project a winning self-image over the phone.

In his book *Time Management for Dummies,* Jeffrey J. Mayer offers the following suggestions for someone in the market for a new computer:

▶ Service is key, probably more important than the equipment itself.

▶ Get the fastest computer on the market and "you'll never be disappointed."

▶ Add lots of random access memory (16 MB or even 32 MB).

▶ Get a huge hard drive (1,000 MB or more).

▶ Put in a fast video card with at least 4 MB of memory.

▶ Get a big monitor (17 or 21 inch).

▶ Get a triple or quadruple speed (or faster) CD-ROM with a good sound card and great speakers.

▶ Get a high-speed modem (28,800 BPS).

▶ Get an automatic back-up system for your hard drive.

▶ Continue to upgrade both your hardware and software so that you always have the best equipment available.

Mayer also recommends equipment that can make your office more ergonomic and efficient, including the following:

▶ A kinesis ergonomic keyboard (800-454-6374).

▶ An Expert mouse trackball (800-535-4242).

▶ A Seiko Smart Label Printer (800-888-0817) for printing single labels.

▶ A Criterion ergonomic chair by Steel Case (800-333-9939).

The first virtue in a soldier is endurance of fatigue.

Napoleon Bonaparte

If you work out of your home, run a small business or are in the job search mode, running errands is a tempting diversion from the real work. Fortunately for your output and unfortunately for your lazy side, many errands can be avoided simply by picking up the phone:

▶ Reliable Office Supply provides next-day delivery of most office supplies and equipment (800-621-4344).

▶ You can order stamps by mail by calling 800-STAMP-4.

▶ Any local florist can send flowers to somebody you feel guilty about not visiting.

Don't get stuck! Any time you bog down, get up and take a walk; start doing something different; exercise; anything that will reinvigorate your attention.

Whenever you're out and about, pretend that you're an action hero in a B-movie, constantly on the lookout for danger. You'll be amazed at how creating this kind of mind-set helps you move through your day with greater efficiency.

There are many courses, books and tape programs on speed reading. Take one or get one and use it.

Do what you have to do when you have to do it.

Don't drop everything when the mail comes in, when you get an e-mail message or when a fax comes through. Reach a natural breaking point first, otherwise, you're letting external interruptions control your day.

Take some time every day to slow down, meditate and wake up, and you'll find yourself getting a lot more done.

Remember the wisdom of the *I Ching* that, as with so much in life, effective time management is not an attainment; it's a maintainment.

Finally, if reading all the books, or perhaps attending a seminar, does not help, you might benefit from the services of a personal coach.

And for me, at least, the fun is in the process . . . . Sure victory is sweet. But it's just a moment . . . . When you're in the process, in the groove of the work itself in all its twists and turns, its mess, its mistakes, the nightmare days and anguished nights when you're working it through—that's sustainable *excitement. It's the journey.*

Barry Diller, Chairman and CEO, Silver King Communications

5

Managing Your Money

A penny saved is no longer a penny earned. With today's tax structure, it's more like two pennies earned. Studies show that people who are in control of their personal finances are more effective in their careers. There are lots of people interested in helping you spend your money, but only you are responsible for managing it. Many companies offer investment savings plans, and some allow you to invest as much as 10 percent of your income and will match part or all of your investment. If you own your own business—even if it's a small business in addition to your regular job—there are advantages to investing in an individual retirement account. At the present rate of savings, many employees won't be able to retire in the style they expect. Don't be one of them.

Prosperity starts with an idea. Become convinced that it's available, persuade yourself to obtain it, and accept it as it arrives. Then, if you're positive about it, you breathe life and form into it.

Mark Victor Hansen and Jack Canfield, *Dare to Win*

If you need no other reason to be on top of your finances, a study of performance by sales representatives conducted at the Cox School of Management of Southern Methodist University in Dallas found that sales reps with greater financial independence achieved higher sale levels. The study's authors conclude that the financially independent group had a greater sense of freedom because they were not so worried about losing the job.

About 2,500 years ago, Lao Tzu said in *Tao Te Ching* that the sage must be ruthless. Want to be a sage of financial management? Learn to be ruthless. When it comes to creating personal wealth, desire management is more important than financial management. Whenever presented with an opportunity to spend money that doesn't directly relate to one of your high-priority goals, Just Say No. Write these three words down on a card and put them in your wallet next to your credit cards. There you have it: *No Brainer Money Management.*

It's imperative that you explicitly understand your philosophy of money. Do you see money as the source of great good or the root of all evil? Is work necessary drudgery, required to pay the bills, or the source of great future potential? Is the world in your eyes a place of poverty or a place of abundance? Do you consider yourself by nature a spender or a saver? Write down in a sentence or two your philosophy of money. Is it consistent with your overall goals in life? Or could your ideas about money (which fundamentally boil down to whether you think you deserve it or not) undermine your ability to achieve your stated goals?

Van K. Tharp, who manages a financial services firm of the same name, tells of a client who suffered from low self-esteem and did not believe himself to be worthy of success. He thought that making money in the stock market would enhance his self-esteem, but continuously sabotaged his performance, because being wealthy wasn't in accordance with his beliefs about himself. Once he changed his self image and accepted his self-worth, his performance improved dramatically.

Here's a list of 10 self-defeating behaviors that can undermine your financial health. Do any apply to you? Can you think of others?

1. Shopping to break a depression.

2. Using mail order or home TV shopping to cope with boredom.

3. Learned helplessness when it comes to understanding finances.

4. Refusing to deal with paperwork and filing; keeping sloppy records.

5. Buying lottery tickets or other gambling.

6. Wasting time on television or other mindless activities.

7. Giving money away without having first evaluated the charity or cause.

8. Believing that the world's resources are scarce, and that you don't deserve any more than you already have.

9. Being impatient and taking a "get rich quick" flyer rather than being willing to accumulate wealth slowly.

10. Not seeking to be compensated at the level for which your time is worth.

Making a list of all possibilities for adding money here and now and getting a part-time job can be very calming. You may need to reorient your thinking to realize that working at McDonalds to pay the mortgage opens rather than limits your possibilities.

Frances Quittel, *Firepower*

Money is a left-brain subject. That is, it's numerical and quantifiable. It's not like beauty in the eye of the beholder; you either have money or you don't. Most of us, however, deal with money in our right brains. We think about it emotionally, and it can raise the basest and noblest of emotions. Consciously discipline your mind to think rationally and to speak precisely on the subject of money. You're more likely to achieve a goal that is worded, "I want to have a million dollars by age 45," than you are to achieve a goal that is worded, "I want to have more money than I'll ever be able to spend."

Jonathan Sabin is the owner of Vortex, and eclectic gift shop in Iowa City, Iowa, that sells wonderful things for the home and office. Sabin teaches about responsibility using don Juan Matus' ideas about the "tonal" and the "nagual," as elaborated upon in the books of Carlos Casteneda. The tonal is the here-and-now, everyday consciousness of our world. The nagual is the subconscious realm of dreams, spirituality, and ultimate transformation. One cannot, says don Juan, truly enter the world of the nagual until they've "cleared the island" of the tonal by accepting personal responsibility for their physical, emotional and financial foundation. On a scale of 1 to 10, how ready are you to accept full responsibility for your finances? If it's anything less than an eight, you've some island cleaning to do.

The iron law of cause and effect applies to money just as powerfully as it does to physics. If you wish to be wealthy, you can cause this to happen by studying and applying the laws of wealth. You can cause yourself to become impoverished by ignoring them. Leaving your fortune to luck or fate is right-brain thinking that makes for great soap operas, but lousy financial planning. Accepting personal responsibility for your financial status requires more discipline and work, but you'll be much happier with the outcome.

◊◊◊

Don't daydream, because dreams aren't real. Rather, create memories of the future. Visualize the future that you would like to have. Clip out pictures of the house, car, vacation spots and other material things you'd like to have in your future world. Speak with people who have gone from where you are now to where you'd like to be, and ask how they did it. Picture yourself doing the same thing. Believe it and you can achieve it. First, though, there will be considerable work and sacrifice, growing in proportion with the size of the dream.

Do a reality check. When it comes to your financial future, are you thinking wishfully—assuming that everything will work out without having rational reason to do so? Are you thinking dreadfully—imagining that everything will go to hell in a handbasket without considering all you can do to prevent this from happening? Instead, try positive thinking. Here's an important distinction: wishful thinking is hoping for something and waiting for it to happen; positive thinking is expecting something and working for it to happen. Create an ambitious but realizable plan, work on it every day, and track your progress toward achieving milestone goals.

Keep track of every cent that comes into or goes out of your life.
Joe Dominguez and Vicki Robin, *Your Money or Your Life*

If you've lost a job or taken a hit in the stock market, don't think about what you've lost. Think about what you've got left. Some of this century's greatest fortunes were made by people who rebounded from tough times, leveraging what they had left to achieve great accomplishments. Make a list of all those things, such as health, imagination, family and friends and material assets that you can use to leverage your way forward.

In his classic book *Think and Grow Rich,* Napoleon Hill expressed the opinion that 85 percent of all failures occur as a result of lack of purpose. You're much more likely to achieve your financial goals if you think not in terms of what the money will buy, but rather in terms of how it will help you achieve your purpose. In an often-cited study of college seniors at Yale University, it was found that only 3 percent had written goals. Twenty years later, that 3 percent had more money than the other 97 percent combined. What are your goals? How do they relate to your central purpose? Write them down for the following 10 categories:

1. Career Growth.
2. Lifestyle.
3. Family.
4. Philanthropy.
5. Housing.
6. Travel/Vacation/Recreation.
7. Investment.
8. Other business opportunities.
9. Retirement expectations.
10. Possessions.

Here are 10 things you can do to quickly accumulate $7,500:

1. Cancel cable and sell your TV.
2. Sell the extra car, or trade down for a smaller car.
3. Eat at home, eat frozen pizza instead of ordering, and drink water instead of soda pop.
4. Check out library books instead of renting videos.
5. Take your annual vacation in the backyard.
6. Pay off credit card debt to reduce interest expense.
7. Moonlight or start a small entrepreneurial business.

8. Cancel magazine, book club and record club subscriptions.

9. Plant a garden, make your own clothes and do your own repairs.

10. Quit an expensive habit, especially if it's something self-destructive like smoking.

Now, here's what to do with that $7,500. Start an all-in-one brokerage account with Charles Schwab (800-548-8100). Use it as your own personal investment laboratory, researching and purchasing stocks and/or mutual funds (the reason for starting at $7,500 is in case the value of some investments falls; if you maintain at least a $5,000 balance, there's no fee). You can access your money via an ATM or checkbook, but don't. Oh, they'll also send you a Visa debit card. Cut it up.

There's a saying on Wall Street that bulls can make money, and bears can make money, but pigs will never make money. One of the great paradoxes of financial life is that people who are too obsessed with monetary gain typically end up self-destructing in one way or another. Honestly examine your own motivations, and purge greed and self-interest; it will pay off in the long run.

Paradoxically, rich societies seem to breed dependence. If you're poor, you're forced into self-sufficiency. As you get rich, it's easier and more sensible to get other people to do what you do not want to do or cannot do. . . . Affluence breeds service industries, and they in turn create affluence.

Charles Handy, *The Age of Unreason*

Understand your personal tolerance for risk. Most people are too conservative (for example, investing only in fixed income securities), and miss out on gains that would occur with more aggressive but still prudent strategies. It's an all too common pattern,

unfortunately, that after years of painstakingly accumulating reserves, they decide to take a flier. More often than not, they fly off
the edge of a cliff. Remember that accumulating money is like
climbing a mountain: the ascent requires planning and preparation
and is long and arduous; an unplanned descent can be precipitous
and quite painful.

If you aren't already using Quicken or a similar computerized
money management system, it may be the most important step
you can take right now. *PC Magazine* says of Quicken 4 for Windows: "Few titles dominate their categories as unfailingly as
Quicken. . . . This year, the proof is concrete, Quicken 4 for Windows sits atop the money-management pile as our sole Editors'
Choice." MECA Software's Managing Your Money for Windows,
with abundant advice from financial guru Andrew Tobias, was
given an honorary mention and rated superior for its tax-planning
capabilities and overall versatility.

Become a little bit obsessive about your money. Set aside 15
minutes or so every evening to enter all income and expenses
for that day on Quicken. Every weekend update the value of your
investments using that Friday's issue of *The Wall Street Journal*.
Using Quicken, prepare reports showing your expenses compared
to budget, investment performance and current net worth. Pat
yourself on the back for progress, but don't panic if things aren't
where you want them to be. Persist with patience and you'll get
there.

Invest in an investment software package like Wealth Builder 4
for Windows from Reality Online, *PC Magazine*'s Editors'
Choice for 1995. This software has historical information on most
stocks and mutual funds, and criteria can be configured to create
screens that can guide your investment decisions. You may or may
not aspire to be an investment wizard, but just playing around with

a program like this can make you a much more knowledgeable and sophisticated steward of your investments. For example, in a matter of seconds you'll be able to find out if the mutual funds that your financial counselor or stockbroker has recommended are dogs or stars.

Remember Adam Smith's memorable comment from the book *The Money Game:* "If you don't know who you are, the stock market is an expensive place to find out." The same could also be said for the bond market, the commodities market, Corporate America, Self-Employed America, Retired America. If you don't know who you are, chances are you're in for an expensive lesson.

Bob Ballard is a 48-year-old Colorado tax attorney who isn't going to retire. Not because he loves his job so much but because he hasn't saved enough and, given his expense and income structure, he may never make it. Ballard isn't alone. According to Stanford Economist B. Douglas Bernheim, the average baby boomer has only one-third of what he or she needs to retire comfortably—less if the social security system fails us.

And, as Brian O'Reilly pointed out in *Fortune* magazine, corporate pensions won't provide as much as they do now since so many companies are trimming back. Banking on an inheritance is also unwise. "The median is only $30,000 per person—enough to pay for about one year in a nursing home for Mom or Dad."

If you're a spendaholic, in over your head in debt or out of control of your finances, consider getting professional help. Possible sources include the employee assistance program where you work, a professional financial advisor (but see the upcoming advice), one of the 1,100 offices of the Consumer Credit Counseling Service (800-388-CCCS), or Debtors Anonymous (212-642-8220). By the way, if you don't think you've got a problem, one of the first symptoms of being in deep trouble is denial. Don't deny problems until you've put Quicken through its paces and been reassured that you're where you need to be to pay the bills, put the kids through school and retire comfortably and on time.

You have to be prudent. Resist the temptation to live beyond your means.

Marvin B. Roffman, *Take Charge of Your Financial Future*

One of the great "how to get rich" classics is George Clason's *The Richest Man in Babylon.* Apply his "Five Laws of Gold" to your financial life and you'll do well:

1. Before you spend a penny of your take-home pay, pull out at least 10 percent to invest for your future.

2. Find profitable sources of investment for your saved money.

3. Be cautious with your investments and get capable advice.

4. Don't invest in businesses or purposes with which you're unfamiliar.

5. Don't demand extraordinary returns because it will lead you into excessive risk.

Instantly squash any dreams you may ever have of winning the lottery, being "discovered" or otherwise hitting the proverbial home run. Remember that lotteries hurt more people than they help, including many of the big winners. Babe Ruth wasn't famous because he hit one home run, but because he consistently hit home runs. Dreams of getting something for nothing or of hitting the big one and being able to stop working will undermine your self-image as a self-reliant individual, not to mention being a waste of your time and creative energy.

*M*oney magazine interviewed four dozen economists, psychologists, investment managers and financial planners to identify eight psychological mistakes people make in dealing with their money:

1. We fear loss more than we should—ACTION: One way to be more rational is to forget about sunk costs and base our thinking only on future risk and reward.

2. We ignore inflation—ACTION: It helps to think in term of buying power instead of absolute dollar.

3. We are intimidated by people perceived to be experts— ACTION: It helps to ignore the conventional wisdom and set your own investment guidelines.

4. We tend to be overconfident when we've got only a little knowledge—ACTION: It helps to keep good records and remember your mistakes as well as your wins.

5. We hear only what we want to hear—ACTION: Seek out contrary opinions and analyze them objectively.

6. We value "easy money" less than "hard-earned" money; for example, being more willing to spend by credit card than with cash—ACTION: When using a credit card, ask yourself if you would be willing to buy the same item with cash.

7. We resist change—ACTION: Remember that not changing is a decision and often a bad one; for example keeping money in the bank because you're not willing to study mutual funds.

8. We bite off more than we can chew—ACTION: Don't buy more than you need, even when it's all part of a "package deal."

*S*peaking of mistakes, here's a list of money mistakes that women commonly make, compiled by Shelby White in the book *What Every Women Should Know about Her Husband's Money:*

1. Putting inherited money or property into a joint account.

2. Using her money for expenses while her husband's investments increase untouched.

3. Not getting professional advice soon enough.

4. Giving up control over her money to show faith and to bolster her husband's ego.

5. Letting her husband keep all the family records.

6. Trying to pay an equal share when she can't really afford to do so.

7. Using her own money to contribute to a joint purchase while her husband's investments are untouched.

8. Not keeping records or receipts, especially for cash payments.

9. And the biggest mistake of all—thinking that talking about money is not romantic and should be avoided.

By systematically setting aside even a small amount of money each week, each payday, or each month, over time you'll have accumulated a significant nest egg.

Tama McAleese, *Get Rich Slow*

And here's *The Wall Street Journal*'s list of "Money Blunders of the Otherwise Intelligent":

1. Not taking charge of money; being intimidated and confused by finances.

2. Buying securities on the basis of a cold call.

3. Buying last year's hot investment.

4. Not watching investments and being prepared to act if they go in the wrong direction.

5. Buying bonds after correctly projecting that interest rates are going up (causing a loss of principle).

6. Incorrectly assuming that fixed income investments will have fixed value; not realizing that changes in interest rates will alter value.

7. Putting excessive faith in the word "guaranteed."

8. Making poor investment decisions strictly for tax reasons.

9. Putting assets in the wrong name.

10. Neglecting to finish the details; for example, setting up a trust and not putting assets into it.

Mark Hulbert, editor of the *Hulbert Financial Digest,* which monitors the performance of financial advisory letters, believes that there are only two major mistakes you can make in investing:

1. Taking on excessive risk. To assess your risk, Hulbert says you should check your portfolio after each rally or correction. "If on average your portfolio loses or gains more than two or three times as much as the market, then chances are high that you're incurring too much risk."

2. The second mistake that most losers make is failure to follow a discipline. "Big losses often can be traced to not having a contingency plan for what to do when investments don't work out as planned." This requires having a plan in advance, and having at least a mental stop-loss point on all of your investments to keep you thinking rationally.

In their book *Your Money or Your Life,* Joe Dominguez and Vicki Robin say that money is just something that you trade your life energy for. This is a profound statement: you aren't trading just your time, but also your emotional, physical and spiritual energy. Joseph Campbell once said that anyone who gets paid for a job they hate is a prostitute. Make a list of things you're trading for the money you get from work; is it worth it?

◈◈◈

Order The Financial Planning Organizer Kit from Homefile ($19.95, by calling 800-695-3453). This is a particularly useful system for filing financial and personal records. It includes a Quick-Find Index that cross-references 200 different kinds of paper.

Your financial plan will be as unique as your thumbprint. There are no right or wrong goals, only ones that excite you because you believe in them.

Mary L. Sprouse, *If Time Is Money, No Wonder I'm Not Rich*

Make sure you're protected if you're out of work. Join AAA, especially if you're driving an older car. Get disability insurance and an umbrella liability insurance policy if you're not covered.

If you're currently out of work or there's at least a 10 percent chance you will be within the next year (and there's at least a 75 percent chance that means you), read my lips: No New Debt. But you should have a credit line at a local lending institution. But make a commitment not to use it except for a bona fide emergency.

Your debts are your enemies, but your creditors are your friends. People to whom you owe money have every reason to want you to succeed. Keep them informed, ask them for advice, get them behind you. Then make an ironclad commitment that you'll pay them back.

Subscribe to *Bottom Line Personal* (P.O. Box 50379, Boulder, Colorado, 80321-0379), which is a wonderful source of summary information on everything from how to take care of your car and find a good vacation spot to managing your money and your career. If you're starting or running a small business, *Bottom Line Business* (P.O. Box 50387, Boulder, Colorado, 80321-0387) can be similarly helpful, providing information and recommendations on such subjects as tax minimization, record-keeping, employee management and facilities maintenance.

B ring home the skills you apply at work. How can you improve productivity in your household? Budget management? Try this: use the principles of open book management with your family. Make sure everyone knows all of the numbers (the good, the bad and the ugly); that they know what each person can do to move the numbers; and what is in it for each of them if they do move the numbers. Have a weekly family meeting to review net worth, budget performance, cash flow and growth in savings (including that highly motivating vacation account).

L everage your capital. One skilled laborer purchased a small acreage in rural Iowa. As he watched "civilization" move closer, he decided to erect a small apartment building on his land. Rent payments more than offset his entire mortgage. Though some of his renters had greater incomes, he enjoyed a higher standard of living.

H ave a jar for "lucky coins." Every time you find a coin on the ground, or (hallelujah!) a greenback, put it in that jar. As you watch it grow heavier, remind yourself that opportunities are everywhere, and that the more lucky coins that you find and pick up, the more seem to show up.

Take a dollar bill and do something that doubles it (like buying a dollar's worth of cookie dough and selling two dollar's worth of cookies). Now you have two dollars; go out and double that. Now go out and double your four dollars. Do this 20 times and calculate what you've got (hint: it's a lot!).

Use dollar cost averaging to build your investment portfolio and minimize your risk. Every month, invest a fixed amount in securities—for example, a growth or aggressive growth mutual fund. By investing the same amount every month, you reduce the emotional roller coaster of Wall Street, and assure that you're buying at least some shares inexpensively. It's easy to link up a mutual fund with automatic withdrawal from your bank account.

Getting involved with a manageable number of companies and confining your buying and selling to these is not a bad strategy. Once you've bought a stock, presumably you've learned something about the industry and the company's place within it, how it behaves in recessions, what factors affect the earnings, etc.

Peter Lynch, *Beating the Street*

Learn about mutual funds. In their book *Smart Money: How to Be Your Own Financial Manager*, Ken and Daria Dolan say that the biggest problem they encounter in their radio and TV talk shows and seminars is that many people don't understand mutual funds, including many who have been investing in them. Most financial and news magazines have an annual performance review of mutual funds. The Wealth Builder computer program allows you to screen mutual funds for a desired level of risk and past performance indicators. The best source of information about mutual funds is MorningStar. You can take out a trial three-month subscription for $55, or obtain the information on a floppy disk for $45 (800-876-5005).

K now what's in the mutual funds in which you've invested. Who's managing them? Performance often suffers after a management change. What specific stocks are being purchased? You can inadvertently increase your exposure to risk by buying a firm with a generic name that behaves like a specialized fund, for example, investing heavily in biotechnology. What is the risk level? A fund may be greatly increasing your risk by investing in options, commodities or other more exotic instruments. What are the hidden costs? A mutual fund manager who makes frequent trades can increase your capital gains taxes.

I n a major change of philosophy last year, *Money* magazine called for "Nothing less than a complete reorientation of your expectations as a fund investor," and recommends that between 45 and 50 percent of your money be invested in index funds. These are mutual funds that strive to track overall market averages as closely as possible. *Money* recommends investing the balance in mutual funds that are actively managed by people who have consistently been able to demonstrate market-beating performance. They say it's the paradox of mutual fund investing today: "Gunning for average is your best shot at finishing above average."

I f you're out of work, most career and outplacement counselors will tell you to treat finding a new job as your full-time job. But here's contrary advice you can take to the bank: if you make mastering the art and science of investment a quarter-time job and leave the rest for the job search, you'll end up better financially, perhaps by hundreds of thousands of dollars—by the time you retire.

Y ou may read advice that you shouldn't follow your stocks or mutual funds too closely, as you might become unnecessarily upset by the daily vicissitudes of the market. Nonsense! If you've followed the advice about understanding your risk tolerance, having an investment plan and managing your emotions, you should be making a discipline of following your investments. Make a game of it. Use Quicken and Wealth Builder to their best benefit.

Reinvest all interest, dividends, capital gains and any other distributions from mutual funds, money market accounts or stock investments. Never let the money come into your mailbox and you'll never miss it; let it continue to compound in your name.

Never, ever take money out of a tax deferred retirement account. Never! You may find that you need to borrow against it, in which case, most of the interest repayments will be to yourself. Get a job delivering newspapers or selling flowers on street corners if that's what it takes to protect your retirement nest egg.

I have observed many successful investors, and they all seem to have three things in place. First, they have a strategy of some sort that gets them into and out of an investment. Second, they have risk or money management concepts that preserve their assets when the investments don't work out the way they thought they would. Third, and most important, they have a good understanding of themselves, and they have structured their investments to suit their situation, resources, and personality.

Thomas F. Basso, *Panic-Proof Investing: Lessons in Profitable Investing from a Market Wizard*

Mark and Kathleen Romeo of San Diego were able to amass a $90,000 portfolio in four years by investing 30 percent of their combined $60,000 income. Both make nondeductible contributions to their IRAs, which are invested in growth-stock funds.

The Romeos will miss the trap that many others have set for themselves. *Money* magazine reports that although 73 percent of adults between the ages of 21 and 64 expect to retire comfortably, with 74 percent planning to do so before the age of 65, less than half are investing in assets likely to provide the money they'll need.

Here's a great reason to do some consulting, freelancing or other outside work for which you earn self-employed income. It will allow you to set up a Keogh retirement plan, which is superior to IRA in several respects, including deductibility of costs regardless of your income level, and higher contribution limits (up to $30,000 a year).

R. Theodore Benna, the man who invented the Individual Retirement Account (IRA) was interviewed by *Bottom Line Personal* about the secrets of a secure retirement. Here is his advice:

▶ Assume that you're going to retire tomorrow, no matter how old you are. That way, every time you're tempted to spend money, you might more seriously consider saving it instead. If you're 40 or older and haven't yet built significant savings, you probably need to be saving 15 percent to 20 percent of your gross income.

▶ Don't expect to receive much from Social Security.

▶ Expect to live much longer than you think you will; the average person who retires today can count on spending about 25 years in retirement.

▶ Expect modest inflation to continue.

▶ Formulate a realistic investment strategy and aim to earn a rate of at least 9 percent per year over the long haul. To do this, a significant part of your investment portfolio needs to be in common stocks or mutual funds.

▶ Try to resist early retirement, which both reduces the amount of your pension payout and extends the number of years over which it must be stretched.

▶ Before starting your own post-retirement business, make sure that you can sustain any potential losses of your capital. Ideally, the business should be up and running and beyond the highest risk stage before you retire.

Here are some phone calls you can make in your retirement planning:

▶ The Labor Department (202-219-9247). Ask for the publication *Top 10 Ways to Beat the Clock and Prepare for Retirement.*

▶ Call Social Security at 1-800-772-1213 to request a free estimate of your benefits.

▶ Request information from the Pension and Welfare Benefits Administration at 202-219-8776.

▶ Request an information packet from The American Association of Retired Persons at 202-434-3525.

▶ Request a packet of information from the Commission on Saving and Investment in America at 202-637-0110.

You, and only you, must take charge of your retirement. If you're unable to retire comfortably, there will be no one to blame but you. It's common knowledge that Social Security will supply only a small fraction of your retirement fund needs. Between 1990 and 1995, 43,000 American corporations converted from defined benefit (where you're paid a known monthly amount upon retirement) to defined contribution (where you're responsible for managing your nest egg, and the quality of your retirement depends on your success as a money manager) pension plans. As Americans live longer, and are less able to rely on outside retirement funding sources, they must take responsibility for their own retirement planning.

Construct a chart of how you spent your money, month by month, over the past six months . . . the more precise the better. You need a detailed picture as a starting point.

Jane Bryant Quinn, *Making the Most of Your Money*

I f you receive a lump-sum severance payment after losing a job, it would be hard to beat this advice: deposit the entire amount into a money market fund, then each month invest one-twentieth of the amount into a blue chip mutual fund (dollar cost averaging an increasingly large investment portfolio, while providing you with a declining cash balance as you, hopefully, get closer to that next job).

W hat do these famous motivational writers and speakers have in common: Norman Vincent Peale, Robert H. Schuller, and Mark Victor Hansen? They, like many other great achievers, truly believe that one who gives will receive in greater measure, and have made tithing—giving 10 percent of their income to charities—a central part of their core personal philosophy. Anthony Robbins, author of *Awaken the Giant Within,* says that the turnaround in his life began the day he gave money he couldn't afford to someone who needed it more. Whether you have great or small income, increase your giving—now. You'll be amazed at the unpredictable return on your investment.

T he most effective way for you to make money tomorrow is to help someone else make money today.

The conventional wisdom is that you shouldn't pay off your home mortgage on an accelerated basis because the interest expense is tax deductible. In many cases, the greater wisdom may be to accelerate the payments so that you've maximum flexibility to capitalize upon future career opportunities or to cope with career setbacks.

Robert J. McCarthy, President of R. McCarthy and Associates Inc, a financial advisory firm in Medfield, Massachusetts, recommends keeping a diary to record all job-search contacts, activities and expenditures. Record the time, place and purpose of all meetings. Keep all receipts covering your expenses. You can deduct many job search expenses including printing, postage, office supplies, publications, transportation, phone and fax, and meetings (unless you're reimbursed by someone else). Even small costs can add up.

Do your taxes as soon as possible after the first of the year. If you owe money, you'll want to know about it as soon as possible. If you've a refund coming, you should be collecting the interest income, not Uncle Sam.

If you want to sell your house, interview many real estate agents. Ask questions, get a sense of the value of your home, ask how they would market it, and what they would do to fix it up. Then begin advertising it as "for sale by owner." Save the 5 to 7% commission. If you're not successful after two or three months, go back to the real estate agent at the top of your list and retain his or her services.

If you feel that you need the services of a financial advisor, look for one in the same way you'd look for a career adviser:

1. Make sure you really do need one.

2. Specify the job description.

3. Set evaluation criteria.

4. Check his or her credentials and make sure that he or she is a certified financial planner.

5. Real Chapter 10 of *Smart Money: How to Be Your Own Financial Manager* by Ken and Daria Dolan.

6. Ask tough questions.

7. Use a fee-only advisor, not somebody who makes a commission selling you insurance or other products.

8. Approve *all* transactions in your account.

The worst investment a person can make is one that he or she does not understand.

> Ken and Daria Dolan, *Smart Money: How to Be Your Own Financial Manager*

Consider starting an investment club. A group of women in Vermont founded The Burlington Stockettes in 1983. They told *Bottom Line Personal* that the club provided three benefits: good returns on their money; an invaluable hands-on course in investing; a support of community of friends working as a team. To learn more about investment clubs, contact the National Association of Investor Corporations, 1515 East 11 Mile Road, Royal Oak, Michigan, 48067, 810-583-6242 PH, 810-583-4880 FAX.

There are lots of great books on investment and financial planning. Here are a few of my favorites:

The Wall Street Journal has a series of extremely user-friendly financial guides by Kenneth M. Morris and Alan M. Siegel (occasionally with other co-authors). These include *Understanding Money and Investing, Understanding Personal Finance, Planning Your Financial Future,* and *Understanding Taxes.* For most of us, these books are a great place to start.

Making the Most of Your Money by Jane Bryant Quinn is as comprehensive, useful, and entertaining a book on personal finance as one could ask for. In some 900 pages, it covers everything from establishing a budget to home ownership to retirement planning.

Smart Money: How to Be Your Own Financial Manager by Ken and Daria Dolan. The question-and-answer format covers all the basics and much advanced information. This book is very readable and a great reference as you do your own financial planning. Here's a tidbit: No matter what kind of pension plan you do or don't have, you should also have an IRA.

Still the Only Investment Guide You'll Need by Andrew Tobias. Here's a key point: For every dollar you spend, you must earn two dollars because of the combined effective state, local and federal taxes.

How to Get Out of Debt and Live Prosperously by Jerrold Mundis. Here's a key point: Make yourself a binding promise that you'll never declare bankruptcy; this will give you the fortitude to keep working, even when you don't feel like it. Whether you think you have a debt problem or not, you should read this book.

Barron's Guide to Making Investment Decisions by Douglas Sease and John Prestbo. If your personal finances are in reasonably good shape, you've a basic understanding of how the economy works, and you've a bit of money to invest, this book is an excellent home study course on the fundamentals of investment.

Recall the earlier suggestion to describe your philosophy of money. At that time, I stated that many people—perhaps most—unnecessarily limit themselves by subconsciously believing that they aren't deserving of money. There is, however, another side to that coin, which is appropriate to reflect upon in closing this chapter on managing your money.

First, as my good friend Brother Michael Crosby said in his book, *The Spirituality of the Beatitudes: Matthew's Challenge for First World Christians,* greed is not good: "To have more than enough is to lack the quality of mercy toward tablemates. Living in excess violates the covenant." That doesn't mean that everyone must be poor, as the poor do not have a very good record of helping the poor, though Mike and I sometimes argue about this—he pointing out that the rich don't have a very good record of helping the poor, either.

Second, the world's resources and the environment in which we live are being exploited at a rate that many scientists believe cannot be sustained. Third, there's a growing realization among the baby boom generation that money indeed doesn't buy happiness. So in setting your goals, aim for enough money to make a difference in your life and in the world, but don't drain your energy trying to grab more than enough; life's too short.

Many "money mystics" speak of the power people have to make money appear through the power of their thoughts—referred to as abundance thinking. Here's one way to prove it to yourself: Volunteer to raise money for the Ronald McDonald House, Junior Achievement or some other worthy charity. This will help you in two ways. First, the experience will help you overcome your anxiety about cold-calling and perhaps help you make valuable new connections. Second, you'll see that money indeed can be created simply through positive and charitable thought.

Whoever loves money never has enough; whoever loves wealth is never satisfied with his income.

Ecclesiastes 6:10, *The Bible*

"Beam me aboard, Scotty."

6

Career Planning

People who wouldn't dream of traveling across the country without a map or going to the grocery store without a list wander through their work lives without knowing where they're going or what they want. As giant corporations shed thousands of jobs through downsizings (killing the concept that job security comes from loyalty and hard work), it's increasingly important for you to make your own career plans rather than let "the company" make them for you.

With so much of our economy afflicted by trivial jobs chasing manipulated wants, with so many of our public institutions replete with drone-like sinecures, there are serious unmet needs— shelter, food, education, health, justice, peace, safety—that go begging for enduring, imaginative and problem-solving attention.

Ralph Nader, *Good Works: A Guide to Careers in Social Change* by Donna Colvin

Have big goals. Millard and Linda Fuller of Habitat for Humanity didn't set out to eliminate poverty housing in their hometown of Americus or their home state of Georgia. No, their goal is "no more shacks." Anywhere. In the whole world. Zen wisdom holds that a good person is one who plants a tree knowing that he or she may never enjoy the shade. Dream of a beautiful future. Be faithful in caring for the young saplings; the shade will be your monument.

A survey by the American Society of Training and Development found that the four top qualities employers want in their people are:

1. Ability to learn.

2. Ability to listen and communicate information.

3. Innovative problem-solving skills.

4. Knowing how to get things done.

Evaluate yourself along each of these parameters. What can you do to get better?

Do what you're good at. Again, if it seems easy, that is okay. There's no rule that says you can only do what you're bad at.
    Edward M. Hallowell and John J. Ratey, *Driven to Distraction*

When Robert Denniston left his job as a regional sales manager for General Electric Medical System in Waukesha, Wisconsin, he had a dream of someday running his own business. He knew, however, that he had much to learn about how small businesses operate. So, as an interim step, he targeted small-to-medium companies for his job search to learn what he needed to know to start his own enterprise more intelligently.

E. F. Schumacher, in his book *Good Work,* spells out three guidelines for what he calls good work (as opposed to "make" work, hateful work, boring work, and so on):

1. It provides necessary goods and services.

2. It enables us to use and perfect our gifts as good stewards should.

3. It allows us to work in service to and in cooperation with other people, thereby surmounting our inborn egocentricity.

Schumacher concludes that this threefold function makes work so central to human existence, that it's impossible to conceive of life at the human level without work. Are you doing "good" work?

Work is love made visible. And if you cannot work with love but only with distaste, it's better that you should leave your work and sit at the gate of the temple and take alms of those who work with joy.

Kahlil Gibran, *The Prophet*

D on't torment yourself with dreams upon which you don't plan to act.

I n 1936, Dorothea Brande wrote in her book *Wake Up and Live!* about what she called "The will to fail." This was, she said, "the intention, often unconscious, to fill life so full of secondary activities or substitute activities that there will be no time in which to perform the best work of which one is capable." In short, a failure to be disciplined with planning your time and concentrating your effort is tantamount to intending to fail.

Life is complex. Each one of us must make his own path through life. There are no self-help manuals, no formulas, no easy answers. The right road for one is the wrong road for another.

M. Scott Peck, *Further Along the Road Less Traveled*

Margo Frey, a Milwaukee-based career counselor, says the biggest problem in most organizations today is the general level of fear. People are putting in longer hours than they want to or agreed to, and are doing it because they fear losing their jobs. Furthermore, people feel that they cannot be themselves, that they must calculate how their actions and statements will be interpreted in light of their job security. This is unfortunate, she says, because now is the time when companies really need creative ideas, and they're not getting them. In your career planning, look for a company that honors individuality and creativity.

Questions are more important than answers. Give yourself half a day of peaceful solitude and make a list of the most important questions in your life.

It's better to make a mistake with the full force of your being than to carefully avoid mistakes with a trembling spirit. Responsibility means recognizing both pleasure and price, making a choice on that recognition, and then living with that choice without concern.

Dan Millman, *Way of the Peaceful Warrior*

Assume that at some point in your career you'll lose your job and be unemployed for a period of time. Begin now to ruthlessly prune expenses, to live as far below your means as possible, with a goal of having at least six months—and preferably one year—of living expenses invested in relatively liquid money market and mutual funds.

Many job seekers begin with a relatively narrow focus, geographically and professionally, and begin to expand only after becoming discouraged. In this market, however, you may be better off to start with a search that is extended beyond your desired locality and industry. With effective networking and use of electronic job-search techniques, it's easier than you may think, and it may yield some pleasant surprises.

There are no menial jobs, only menial attitudes.

William J. Bennett, *The Book of Virtues*

In their book, *The Discipline of Market Leaders,* Michael Treacy and Fred Wiersema describe how companies tend to focus on a single important cultural value. It may be easier, they suggest, for an employee at Nordstroms, the department store where excellent customer service receives a high premium, to make the transition to a top-tier Cadillac dealership than it would be for someone who's made a living selling Yugos. Make sure there's a fit between your personality and the culture of any organization for which you go to work.

Here's the best advice you'll ever receive on long-range career planning: Consider yourself to be a corporation of one, with you serving as chief executive and senior strategist. As president of "Me, Inc." think of yourself as being responsible for developing long-range strategic plans, continuously improving your product, making marketing contacts, conducting customer research and assuring cash flow to keep the doors open.

Begin with the end in mind.

Stephen R. Covey, *The Seven Habits of Highly Effective People*

If you've never had a job in sales, maybe this is the time to try it—especially if it's the last thing in the world you think you want to do. If you take it seriously, working in sales can give you invaluable skills for the twenty-first century, and boost your self-confidence. It can also keep you from becoming isolated and going broke while you're looking for another job.

A favorite saying of General Electric CEO Jack Welch is: "Control your destiny or someone else will." Who is controlling your destiny?

Would you be willing to do something very unsatisfying (for example clean toilets) for five years if you were certain that the experience would afterwards bring you a deep sense of personal fulfillment for the rest of your life?

Gregory Stock, *The Book of Questions*

The study of history can help you shape your own career success. In my *Success Warrior* seminar, I describe how people can apply these 12 Principles of Military Strategy to their own career management and job search:

1. *The Courage Principle:* The field of battle, said Wu-Ch'i in his 2,500 year old tract on the art of war, is a land of the living dead: those determined to die will live, and those who hope to escape with their lives will die. This is the central paradox that faces many American workers: those whose greatest

hope is to cling to a job until they retire may never find security. Attack your work as an adventure, experience the exhilaration of the struggle, and enjoy the only security that a person can find in this world—security in yourself.

2. *The Mission Principle:* In his classic book *Think and Grow Rich,* Napoleon Hill said that 85 percent of all failures result from not having a sense of purpose. In military history, there's no better example than Hannibal Barca, who for more than 20 years terrorized the Roman countryside, defeating one Roman general after another in some of history's most beautifully executed tactical battles. Yet Hannibal ultimately failed because he did not have a mission beyond beating the Roman legions in battle, as his father had indoctrinated him to do since birth. When the Romans found in Scipio Africanus a commander of greater vision, Carthage was defeated. Write down your mission statement, then build your goals around it. You'll be more likely to achieve them if they are mission-driven.

3. *The Optimism Principle:* The turning point in the American Civil War occurred when President Lincoln found in Generals Grant and Sherman men who *believed* that they could beat the enemy. The career warrior knows that he or she will build tomorrow's reality on the foundation of today's belief, and consciously works to make those beliefs constructive and optimistic. Optimism can be learned; expect the best outcome and you'll likely get it.

4. *The Anticipation and Preparation Principle:* Five different plans were developed for the allied invasion of Normandy; it was the fifth plan that was actually implemented. To be a successful career warrior, cultivate an intelligence network; know what you're looking for and know how to find it; learn how to discern the true nature of reality through the fog of events; understand organizational politics and psychology; create a written battle plan; and understand the goals and strategies of your "enemy," which in the career wars means anyone that can block the achievement of your goals.

5. *The Target Principle:* Early in their military careers, both Napoleon and Hitler showed true genius at having many

enemies, but being able to target them sequentially. Later in their careers, they were each to illustrate the dangers of violating the principle when they lost their focus and extended themselves on multifront wars. Focus means having a limited number of priorities; concentration means applying all available resources to those priorities. The career warrior targets a manageable number of goals, then concentrates everything on their achievement.

6. *The Speed Principle:* General George Patton said that a partially developed plan violently executed is superior to a perfect plan a week too late. Increase your productivity by pruning away unnecessary tasks, and by picking up the pace at which you work, and you'll be amazed at what you can accomplish.

7. *The Pursuit Principle:* One of the things that made the Mongol hoards such fearsome warriors was that they attacked their enemies in waves. First came heavy cavalry, wielding lances and hooks, to serve as shock forces. Immediately behind swarmed several waves of mounted archers pouring murderous volleys into the enemy. If you want to be a success, learn to create and sustain momentum. Attack every problem with more force than required, maintain standards higher than expected, and persevere beyond what's reasonable, and you cannot help but succeed.

8. *The Mobility Principle:* "In strategy" wrote military historian B. H. Liddell Hart, "the longest way round is often the shortest way home." For the career warrior, mental mobility often means maneuvering around old problems in new and unique ways. If you're not making satisfactory progress toward the achievement of your long-range goals and objectives, consider whether you need to make a detour and approach them from a different direction.

9. *The Resiliency Principle:* "I shall return." Douglas MacArthur refused to accept defeat. The career warrior must learn to bounce back, learn from failure, and see the opportunities in adversity. This is the way to make defeat the springboard for greater victory. Think of MacArthur when a rejection letter threatens to ruin your day.

10. *The Security Principle:* The Roman legions never stopped for the night without entrenching themselves into a defensible position. In business or in a career, as in war, you must first survive before you can prevail. Your security comes from continuous learning and innovation; cultivating a strong personal work ethic; creating a broad network of allies; being alert and mindful of danger, even in times of apparent security; building a strong financial foundation; exercising impeccable ethical behavior; minimizing mistakes; and insuring yourself against catastrophic failure or loss.

11. *The Reality Principle:* Hitler thought he could hold continental Europe, bomb Britain into submission, take Moscow, and secure the Balkans all at once. The career warrior learns to avoid such delusional thinking by relentlessly questioning his or her interpretation of reality, seeking continuous 360 degree feedback, and disciplined questioning of "facts" and assumptions. Relentlessly seek to understand the true nature of every situation.

12. *The Leadership Principle:* If one knows the character of two opposing leaders, said Sun Tzu, one can accurately predict which leader will win in combat. The career warrior consciously uses influence to build a team of supporters; develops a strong personal foundation of character and integrity; is willing to make and pursue tough decisions; creates a larger vision; motivates and inspires people; and shows caring and compassion in every action.

If you've got a pretty good idea of the kind of job you want, the book, *The Overnight Job Change Strategy* by Donald Asher, president of Resume Righters in San Francisco, will provide excellent strategies for developing job leads, penetrating corporate defenses and succeeding in the interview and negotiating process. Asher defines a number of "performance standards" which, if you hold yourself to them, will help you push ahead in your job search. These include:

1. Almost immediately generate several dozen job leads, with a goal of compiling a list of 100 percent of employers with the potential to hire you.

2. "Build a big lead list," he says, "and plan on contacting several companies simultaneously, not just one at a time."

3. Call every potential lead at least once per day for seven business days before you abandon it; be thick-skinned and persistent.

4. Return every single phone message the same day you get it.

5. Always call to confirm your interviews, and show up exactly five minutes early.

6. After every interview, immediately write a summary and thank you notes or letters.

Throughout the book, Asher emphasizes these three tenets to guide and drive your search: 1. No technique works 100 percent of the time; 2. No one application or rejection should define your job search; 3. Your goal is to improve your odds on *every* application.

There's no hope of success for the person who does not have a central person, or definite goal at which to aim.

Napoleon Hill, *Think and Grow Rich*

Also by Donald Asher is *The Foolproof Job-Search Workbook,* which is a great resource for someone involved in or planning for a job search. In seven chapters, it walks you through the basics of setting up a job-search command center, self-assessment, identifying job targets, preparing a resume, networking and interviewing. The worksheets are comprehensive and will help you with every phase of the job search process.

S tuds Terkel opened his classic book *Working* with these lines:

> This book, being about work, is, by its very nature, about vio-
> lence—to the spirit as well as to the body . . . . It's, above all (or
> beneath all), about daily humiliations . . . . It's about a search,
> too, for daily meaning as well as daily bread, for recognition as
> well as cash, for astonishment rather than torpor; in short, for a
> sort of life rather than a Monday through Friday sort of dying.

Compare these disheartening words with the following passage
from David Whyte's book *The Heart Aroused: Poetry and the
Preservation of the Soul in Corporate America:*

> Work is the very fire where we are baked to perfection, and like
> the master of the fire itself, we add the essential ingredient and
> fulfillment when we walk into the flames ourselves and fuel the
> transformation of ordinary, everyday forms into the exquisite
> and the rare.

Your attitude determines whether your work is about daily hu-
miliation or the exquisite and the rare.

*Ignore the ones who say it's too late to start over. Disregard
those who say you'll never amount to anything. Turn a deaf ear
to those who say you aren't smart enough, fast enough, tall
enough, or big enough—ignore them.*

Max Lucado, *He Still Moves Stones*

I n a *Fortune* magazine article entitled "The End of the Job,"
William Bridges described seven old rules that one should be
willing to break in this new world in which corporations no longer
provide long-term security to even the most loyal and dedicated
workers:

Old Rule #1: Don't leave your job when other jobs are scarce.
New Rule: If a good opportunity comes along, that may be the
best time to leave your old job.

Old Rule #2: The best jobs go to the people with the best qualifications. *New Rule:* Desire, ability, temperament and other assets are as important if not more so.

Old Rule #3: Getting into the right business assures a secure future. *New Rule:* Being willing to move into what is *currently* the right business assures a secure present.

Old Rule #4: Don't try to change careers after 40. *New Rule:* After age 40 may be the best time to start "You, Inc." You'll be subject to much less age discrimination than is likely if you work for "Someone Else, Inc."

Old Rule #5: What the company wants matters most to your career future. *New Rule:* What the customer wants matters most to your career future.

Old Rule #6: You have to have good sales skills to get ahead. *New Rule:* You have to believe in your product to be effective at sales.

Old Rule #7: If you have financial responsibilities, you had better not leave the world of jobs. *New Rule:* The real risk is not looking ahead to a future where there might not be jobs at all.

If you're considering a major career change, take steps to prepare yourself. You may need to ask whether a given lifestyle or a satisfying career is more important to you. It may be necessary, for example, to dramatically reduce your material expectations—at least in the short term—in order to achieve career fulfillment. Prepare a budget; understand your capital structure; and establish priorities.

Some people today suggest that this search for meaning and identity has resulted from having too many choices, rather than too few. Instead of becoming a gateway to freedom, our wealth of options tether us to a dilemma. And this conundrum echoes through our leisure and free time experiences.

Martin Kimeldorf, *Serious Play: A Leisure Wellness Guidebook*

Phil Lamb lost his job as chief executive officer of a community savings bank in Springfield, Massachusetts. He moved to Cape Cod for a similar job, only to have that eliminated in a corporate reorganization. He says now that the most important lesson he's learned is that it's more important to find personally rewarding work than it is to climb the corporate ladder. Love your work, not your title.

The best time to leave a party is when everyone is having a good time. That's the advice of Cindy Suopis, director of recruitment and staffing for Baystate Health Systems in Springfield, Massachusetts. If everything is going right in your job, consider how much more upside potential there is compared with how quickly and how far things might fall. If you're near the pinnacle, you might want to leave before somebody pushes you.

If there's one common mistake in marketing yourself, it's setting a personal goal and then failing to see other possibilities as they develop.

Al Ries and Jack Trout, *Horse Sense*

It's a great place to start. Tim Letendre joined the U.S. Army in 1984 to make money for college. He ended up staying and working on a bachelor's degree. Although he plans to stay for the 20-year minimum for retirement, he's already planning for the future, trying to figure out how he can make best use of the leadership training that's been provided by the service. It's never too early to start planning for such an important transition, he believes.

D r. David Noer, senior vice president at the Center for Creative Leadership in Greensboro, North Carolina, suggests involving family, friends and peers in the development of your personal mission statement. He tells of one manager who had his wife sign the mission statement, which was then displayed on the wall as a reminder to them both.

Allow careers to unfold as they will. At ad agency Chiat/Day, a secretary might decide to get into the creative side of things— and if she's willing to put in the hard labor, she can then proceed to move in that direction. Why not? Allowing—and encouraging—literally everyone to go where their passion and curiosity take them is important.

Tom Peters, *The Pursuit of WOW!*

I n their book *First Things First,* Stephen R. Covey, A. Roger Merrill and Rebecca R. Merrill list the following attributes of an empowering mission statement:

▶ It represents the deepest and best of your inner life.

▶ It's an expression of your unique gifts and capacity to contribute.

▶ It reflects a mission that is higher than simple satisfaction of personal wants.

▶ It reflects fulfillment in the physical, social, mental and spiritual dimensions.

▶ It's based on principles that enhance true quality of life.

▶ It deals with both character and competence—what you want to be and what you want to do with your life.

▶ It balances the significant roles in your life—personal, family, work, community.

▶ It's written to inspire you, not to impress someone else.

Appendix A of their book includes a "Mission Statement Workshop" that can help you craft your own mission statement.

If you're going to make a major change in direction, prepare yourself for a period of time alone for study, reflection and homework. Winston Churchill once said that anyone who desires to make significant changes must first spend time in "the desert." Listen to the silence of solitude; you might be surprised at what you hear.

You need to have more than one goal for your time of unemployment.

Richard Nelson Bolles, *What Color Is Your Parachute?*

An article in *The Wall Street Journal* by Fred R. Bleakley reported that many career counselors are beginning to offer out-of-work managers what would once have been considered radical advice: "Forget traditional notions about hunting for a job. Rather than seeking a specific job title in a specific industry, learn to be flexible enough to take advantage of whatever opportunities come along." This may mean, Bleakley writes, being willing to relocate, to enter a new industry or skill, to accept a job paying less money or begin further down the totem pole.

Gloria Bjerk with Lee Hecht Harrison Inc. in Bloomington, Minnesota, reports that working with a job-search support group can greatly increase job-search productivity. Group members are able to support each other emotionally, share leads and information, and avoid becoming insular. Bjerk notes that team members tend to land faster and in more appropriate positions than nonteam members.

Probably the most fundamental choice you have to make in the strategic job targeting stage is whether you want your next job to be just that—a job—or whether you want it to be either the first step in a career you want to break into or the next logical step in a career that you've already begun to pursue.

Max Messmer, *Job Hunting for Dummies*

In his book, *Beat the Odds,* Martin Yate suggests pursuing three careers simultaneously. First is your "core career," the job that gives you a steady paycheck and teaches you valuable basic business skills. The second is an "entrepreneurial career," a little business you start up in your spare time—perhaps moonlighting with an existing firm to begin with—that provides you extra money and helps you learn entrepreneurial skills that will be essential in the future. The third is a "dream career," that work which you would love to pursue for your own fulfillment. It's not as unrealistic as you might think, he says. The key is to develop practical know-how that can be applied in multiple different fields.

Chuck Offenburger is recognized by three million Iowans as "The Iowa Boy," his byline for the state's largest newspaper, *The Des Moines Register.* As a reporter, he is in "search" mode all the time, looking for good stories. Anyone involved in career planning or job search can learn from Offenburger's basic philosophy of reporting:

1. Get out of the office.

2. Be interested in lots of different subjects.

3. Learn to be a collector and a teller of stories of real people, because people love stories.

4. Don't be afraid to ask for help.

5. Be true to your real values.

6. When you feel embattled, stay active and help other people rather than turning inward.

7. Keep your eye open for opportunities, because they're always there, but not always obvious.

You can't succeed if you don't fail sometimes. But if you're not prepared for failure, it's going to take you by surprise and knock you for a loop. So you have to manage with the understanding that things may not work out according to plan. You have to have your strategy backed up. The secret is to make contingency planning a habit of mind.

Jack Stack, *The Great Game of Business*

According to Thorndike Deland Associates, a New York executive search firm, 80 percent of retailers are seeking different leadership skills today than they were 10 years ago, while 52 percent expect the company to fill future CEO openings with outsiders. In many ways, the barriers between industries are breaking down. Actively seek ways to learn how to transfer your skills to new industries and to develop new transferable skills.

James LaMorgesse is a 52-year-old neurosurgeon practicing in Cedar Rapids, Iowa. He also is a student of management. He has committed one evening a week to earning a master's degree in health services administration, and is an avid reader of business books. He's already started looking at how his own group practice operates with a new perspective. When the day comes that it's time for him to leave behind the physical demands of nuerosurgical practice, he'll be ready for whatever comes next.

Small companies can provide the best environment for someone who's a bit of a nonconformist, who has a natural creative bent, and who wants to feel in command of his or her own destiny.

R. Linda Resnick, *A Big Splash in a Small Pond: Finding a Great Job in a Small Company*

One advantage of working at a small company is this: there's no upper-level manager who can increase his or her year-end bonus by taking a meat cleaver to the organization chart.

In their book, *The Telecommuter's Handbook: How to Earn a Living without Going to the Office,* Deborah and Brad Schepp describe the characteristics of successful telecommuters. They must have a high level of self-motivation, discipline and excellent time-management skills. Don't do it, they say, to get away from co-workers you don't like, to reduce your work load or because you can't find daycare.

Fate cannot be changed; otherwise it would not be fate. Man, however, may well change himself, otherwise he would not be man.

Viktor E. Frankl, *The Will to Meaning*

If you do consider telecommuting, however, be aware of the dangers. James E. Challenger, president of Challenger, Gray and Christmas, Inc., a Chicago-based outplacement firm, warns that telecommuters can become invisible. He recommends that they keep a presence in the office by attending all meetings and special events, delivering reports in person and finding other reasons to visit the office, keeping supervisors informed—in person—of their progress, keeping up with office memos and mail and being easy to reach (for example, with pagers and answering machines).

Try moving to a hot spot. For example, Los Angeles is the world capital of the entertainment industry. Americans spend more money on entertainment than on cars, and the rapid consolidation that's occurring between the entertainment, information and communications industries will create enormous opportunities. Go to where the action is if what you want is action.

Of all the ways to create work one is more crucial to our time than all the others. It's crucial because it has been most roundly neglected during the industrial era. I am speaking of ritual.

Matthew Fox, *The Reinvention of Work*

To get a fix on where jobs will be in the future, visit your local library and review these documents from the Bureau of Labor Statistics: *Career Guide to Industries,* and the more detailed *Occupational Outlook Handbook,* which profiles 250 different occupations. If you want your own copies, you can order them ($14 and $23, respectively) from the Bureau of Labor Statistics, Publication Sales Center, P.O. Box 2145, Chicago, Illinois, 60690, 312-353-1880.

Make optimal use of computer technology. Nidia Palomo was laid off from her job as a quality engineer. She wasn't confident she could create a secure corporate future, so she decided to do what she loved—become an artist. She had been playing with computer art, and decided to create her business in that field. She used a spreadsheet to analyze potential hardware and software purchases, playing out various combinations that would meet her requirements. She used database software to keep track of people in her field. Her business is now thriving in Caguas, Puerto Rico.

If you're to succeed, you must understand that your rewards in life will be in direct proportion to the contribution you make.

David McNally, *Even Eagles Need a Push*

Outsource yourself. Steve Medici was director of employee benefits at CS First Boston in New York. The investment banking firm was about to outsource the function to a consulting firm, so Medici offered to form an independent company to provide benefits administration. Today his firm, Black Mountain Management Inc., has a five-year contract to administer First Boston's benefits, and is actively seeking other work. All 10 members of the benefits department joined Black Mountain, so no one lost a job.

Sometimes, work itself can be a de facto planning process. Gilda Carle, Ph.D., is president of InterChange Communications Training Inc., and a professor of business management at Mercy College in New York. She started a monthly newsletter with advice about how to project a power image, and mailed it to about 1,000 people. A women's newsletter subsequently asked her to write a monthly column. That attracted the attention of a local TV station producer, who suggested turning the advice into public service advertisements. After that happened, talk shows that had previously rejected her proposals began to call. Last year, she did more than 100 talk shows. If you've got a good idea, follow it all the way.

Everybody battles for success; too few people are aware of its profound impact. Success tends to breed arrogance, complacency and isolation. Success can close a mind faster than prejudice. Success is fragile, like a butterfly. We usually crush the life out of it in our efforts to possess it.

Max DePree, *Leadership Jazz*

Don't love your job too much. Mike Synar was a congressman from Oklahoma for 16 years. "If you think in terms of having your job forever," he used to say, "you won't be willing to take risks." During his tenure, Synar took on multiple special interests including tobacco, the gun lobby, big hospitals and western grazers, in trying to serve the people. He "lost his job" in the conservative landslide of 1994. He then launched what he considered to be three full-time jobs—working for campaign finance reform, chairing a bankruptcy study group and serving as an ambassador to an international telecommunications union. Sadly, Synar recently lost his battle with brain cancer at age 45.

According to James Gallagher, chairperson of The Outplacement Institute in San Rafael, California, a good career counselor will channel and challenge your thinking. He or she will not give you easy answers. The expertise of a career counselor is to help you express problems in a way that they can be solved (for example, not "I need a job," but rather "here's what I would really like to do"); and second, to help you develop an algorithm for solving the problem.

Structure cannot be avoided. If you don't create your own structure, you have to deal with someone else's.
        Laurence G. Boldt, *Zen and the Art of Making a Living*

Before paying for the services of a career counselor, do as much work as you can on your own by reading, networking, attending support groups and free or low-cost workshops (such as those listed at the end of the *National Business Employment Weekly*). If you do get a counselor, check with the National Board for Certified Counselors (800-398-5389) for a list of certified counselors in your area, and check references from previous clients.

In career counseling, you may identify the need for additional education. Mitch Messer, managing director of The Academia Group, says his consortium sees lots of recently divorced women who must now reenter the workforce. Many of them, he says, begin with career counseling to identify what they want to do, and then pursue more formal education in order to get the skills to do it.

Whatever you do, you should want to be the best at it. Every time you approach a task, you should be aiming to do the best job that's ever been done at it, and not stop until you've done it. Anyone who does that will be successful and rich.

Advertising genius David Ogilvy

Here are a variety of things to consider if you're an internal candidate for a job:

1. Conduct an honest self-assessment: Do you really want the job and why?

2. Can you do the job without hitting the Peter Principle?

3. Do you have internal support for your candidacy?

4. Are you a serious candidate?

5. Learn as much as you can about the search firm that is involved, if there is one.

6. Don't assume anything.

7. Complete a resume and cover letter explaining why you want the job as thoroughly as if the addressee were a total stranger.

8. Buy a new suit or two.

9. Put together a dynamite set of references for the time when you're asked to provide them.

10. Develop a business plan that outlines what you would do in your first year and five years on the job.

11. Be visible. Spend lots of time walking around, talking with people, and especially listening.

12. Start acting as if you already had the job.

13. Do some things that surprise people with your energy and initiative.

14. Study. Become an expert in the job, the company and the industry.

15. Spend time networking with the group of people who would be your peers in the new job. This will help you anticipate the questions that will arise, and give your job search a head start should you be unsuccessful.

16. Don't worry about the other candidates; be your best on your own.

17. Prepare for every public exposure as though you were going to be on stage.

18. Consciously manage your thoughts and emotions.

19. Consider whether you should ask for a formal severance agreement if you don't already have one, just in case.

20. Get other people to buy into your success.

If you consider that, in many respects, you're a product trying to market yourself, you can get lots of good ideas from reading the *Guerrilla Marketing* books by Jay Conrad Levinson, and/or by subscribing to his newsletter *Guerrilla Marketing International*. To subscribe, call 800-748-6444.

Almost as many individuals fail because they try to do too much as fail because they do not do enough.

J. Paul Getty, *The Golden Age*

In your planning, ask yourself the following questions:

If all jobs paid the same, what would I be doing?

What would I do if I knew I could not fail?

Remember that nature doesn't evolve toward goals, but away from constraints. You have to consciously push yourself toward your goals.

In his book, *The End of Work,* Jeremy Rifkin argues that in the not-too-distant future, many jobs will have disappeared, leaving most of us unemployed and available for work on nonprofit causes. If you buy into that argument, start now considering what cause you'd like to pursue to make your living in that future.

The fundamental career choice is not between one company and another, but between specializing and generalizing.

Thomas A. Stewart, *Fortune*

Plan for retirement, but don't start dreaming about it. The danger is that your subconscious mind, which is usually not very good about delaying gratification, may begin to think and act in retirement mode prematurely.

Be realistic about money. Investment expert Gordon K. Williamson points out that a 55-year-old earning $70,000 with 25 years seniority under a typical retirement plan retiring at age 55 would get $13,922 per year; at age 60 would get $30,460; and at age 65 would get $45,355. Putting off retirement also allows you to add to your savings.

Mark L. Ferris of Wilcox Financial in Toledo, Ohio, says early retirees generally find the financial side of their new situation to be one of high anxiety. Nevertheless, he says, he has yet to see an early retiree go through the process and regret the decision. He helps early retirees develop financial plans by:

▶ Identifying all sources of immediate income.

▶ Examining the family lifestyle.

▶ Evaluating the family's debt structure.

▶ Realistically and critically examining the potential of the new situation.

Ferris commonly sees people overestimate what their new income potential will be and underestimate the time it takes to generate income.

Positive thinking is working for something and expecting it to happen; wishful thinking is hoping for something and waiting for it to happen.

Rafe, in *Never Fear, Never Quit*

Michael Ginsberg, regional research coordinator for outplacement consultants Right Associates in Philadelphia, suggests considering the job search as being self-employed with deferred income. He recommends the "chutzpah" approach to get yourself energized for the job search and subsequent employment:

Creativity.

Heart.

Uniqueness.

Tenacity.

<u>Z</u>eal.

<u>P</u>ositive <u>A</u>ttitude.

<u>H</u>ired.

I f you're in job search mode from the platform of an existing job, make sure that your office phone is always answered in a polite and cheerful way, and that you're assured of quickly getting your messages.

Lay plans for the accomplishment of the difficult before it be-comes difficult; make something big by starting with it when it's small. Be as careful at the end as at the beginning and there will be no ruined enterprises.

Lao Tzu, *Tao Te Ching*

I f you're interested in working outside of the United States, have a career counselor administer the assessment tool, Overseas Assignment Inventory (OAI), which evaluates your overseas potential, including your flexibility for tolerating other cultures.

ELECTRONIC JOB SEARCH

F or 25 years, Richard Nelson Bolles has been saying that the mechanism for linking job hunters with jobs is broken. As you read this, a revolution is underway that will radically restructure the system. Whether, from your perspective, it fixes it or makes it infinitely worse will depend on your willingness to learn to use the new tools of job search: your personal computer, your modem and the online world.

I think the time has come now when we should attempt the boldest moves, and my experience is that they are easier of execution than the more timid ones.

General William Tecumseh Sherman

According to William J. Morin, former chairman of Drake Beam Morin Inc., the New York-based outplacement firm, nearly 15 percent of DBM's clients are now getting jobs from computerized job banks, compared with only 2 percent five years ago.

The Online Career Center, a nonprofit organization supported by more than 200 member companies, provides information on jobs and careers, company profiles, job listings, a resume database and access to other Internet career resources. The center experiences more than four million visits every month.

There are lots of books available about online job searching. As of this writing, the two best are probably *Be Your Own Headhunter Online* by Pam Dixon and Sylvia Tiersten, and *Finding a Job on the Internet* by Alfred Glossbrenner. These books are complementary, so for the fastest head start, read both.

The courage to risk the disapproval of others, while at the same time going through the doubt of self-examination, is rare. When we begin to examine ourselves, we feel most insecure. It's then that we most look for approval. Finding none, many abandon the quest. This is the time for courage and perseverance.

Laurence G. Boldt, *Zen and the Art of Making a Living*

If you're already an adept Netizen, and all you need is reference information for career services, order *The Job-Seekers Guide to Online Resources* by Alice Snell ($12.95, Kennedy Publications, 800-531-0007). This book provides detailed information on major online services, resumes databases, online job postings, bulletin board services and specialty and miscellaneous other services.

To access a new service being provided by a coalition of the nation's largest newspapers, type careerpath.com on the World Wide Web. This is an interactive employment service that allows job searchers to look for out-of-town jobs quickly and inexpensively.

Contact The University of Michigan Career Planning and Placement Office and request a copy of their report "Job Search and Employment Opportunities: Best Bets From the Net," by Philip Ray and Bradley L. Taylor, which are the best employment-related resources, "either because of their comprehensiveness; their ability to serve the needs of a particular discipline; their ease of navigation; their timeliness; or, the overall quality of the resource." (313-764-7460; fax: 313-763-9268).

John Blakely got his job as a designer of digital multimedia products at Magnet Interactive Studios by responding to an ad on the E-span database. Now, as director of software engineering, he regularly scans Internet newsgroups looking for potential recruits.

Does your dream, the dream you're now committed to, have a transcendent quality? That's important. Dreams that are grand, dreams that others don't think you can handle, dreams that require you to stretch and grow, dreams that demand every ounce of your resources and your energy—these are the dreams

*that inspire and motivate you to keep going when the road gets
rocky, muddy, mucky, when it turns into a quagmire that threatens to swallow you up—and when it disappears from view, leaving you alone in the void.*

Burt Dubin, producer of the Speaking Success System

"Miss Heywood, bring me a screwdriver, a hacksaw, some wire cutters and a plastic garbage bag."

7

Research

Knowledge is power, and the way you get knowledge is through research. In fact, effective research can be more important to your job-search success than a drop-dead resume or great interviewing skills. Befriend the research librarian at your local library and become a voracious reader. Cruise the Internet. Learn how to ask questions that could change your life and career for the better.

In most instances, the one activity that has more bearing than any other on how quickly you find a good job—apart from your qualifications—isn't what most people think. It's not how solid your resume is or how brilliantly you write your cover letters. It's not how drop-dead marvelous you look when you go on interviews. And it's not how smoothly and convincingly you answer interview questions. What it is, in a word, is research.

Max Messmer, *Chairman, Robert Half International*

In his classic work on military strategy, *The Art of War,* which was written in about 350 B.C., Sun Tzu said:

Know the enemy, know yourself; your victory will never be endangered. Know the ground, know the weather; your victory will then be total.

This is the best advice you'll ever receive for a job search. First, know the enemy: that is, anyone with the power to prevent you from reaching your goal of a particular job—gatekeepers within the company, and competing job searchers being foremost among these. Know yourself, and the value you can bring to the organization, as well as weaknesses they'll see which you must overcome. Know the ground: the competitive marketplace in which the target corporation operates. Know the weather: the overall political and economic climate to which the organization must adapt. Know those things and your job search victory will be total.

In his book *101 Corporate Haiku,* William Warriner captures the delicious paradox of all change, including job search, with the following:

> My task is to go
> where no one has gone before—
> and invent the wheel.

In your job search research, learn as much as you can from others so that you don't have to reinvent the wheel. But then, think creatively, so that you can invent a wheel of your own.

Call the Harry W. Schwartz Bookshops in Milwaukee at 800-236-7323 and ask for their compilation of business and marketing books; it's one of the best and most widely read in the country.

Develop a system to organize your research and use it religiously. The Executive Scan Card System is marketed as a project organizer that uses customized index cards and a special binder to track projects. The system can be easily adapted to the job search. For product information, call 800-848-2618.

D r. M. Scott Peck, author of *The Road Less Traveled* and other bestsellers, says that he tends to do his writing first, and do the supporting research later. This isn't a bad idea for the job search, either. The more time you spend up front thinking about the ideal job and the ideal company, writing cover letters to the (yet to be discovered) perfect boss and visualizing that happy first few weeks on the new job, the more targeted and effective your research will be.

There are two great advantages to using government analysts for industry insights. First, they are very willing to help you find the information you need. Second, in many cases, they are the most knowledgeable and impartial sources of information that you'll find.

Leila K. Kight, *Getting the Lowdown on the Job Market and a Leg Up on Employers*

H ere are 12 ways to discover new fields of work:

1. Temporary employment.

2. Consulting.

3. Freelance work.

4. Networking.

5. Volunteer work.

6. Reading books and journals.

7. Computer bulletin boards.

8. Window shopping.

9. Travel.

10. Reviewing want ads.

11. Taking educational courses.

12. Daydreaming.

Find an industry in which you'd like to work and learn everything you can about it and the companies in it. Then plan to write a research paper. Try to get an expression of interest in publishing your paper from an appropriate journal. Then call key people for interviews, offering to send them a prepublication copy of your report when it's finished. People who would not speak with you about your job search may well participate in a research project, especially if there's a prospect that they might gain new knowledge.

Never ask about job openings, but if you're thoroughly prepared and make enough calls, you probably won't need to. Someone on your list will recognize that a person of your get-up-and-go could make a real contribution to his or her organization. Once you've got that new job, your research project will have given you a great start on building your new network.

Read *The 100 Best Companies to Work for in America* by Robert Levering and Milton Moskowitz and see the qualities they regard as essential. Benchmark your target corporations against the best.

Patrick J. Spain, an editor of *Hoover's Handbook of American Business,* suggests the following sources of research information on target corporations:

▶ Annual reports.

▶ 10 Ks (which includes year-end employment figures and competitor information not in the annual report).

▶ Proxy statements prepared for the annual meeting of shareholders (which you can attend if you own stock), which include data on the company's ownership and executive and director compensation.

▶ IPO or S-1 reports for companies recently gone public.

Buy 10 or so shares of stock in any company you're seriously considering for employment. This will put you on the mailing list for their annual report and other materials. It will also give you ready access to their investor relations department (you can call as a shareholder, not a job searcher). If you don't think that the stock is a good investment, why on earth would you consider going to work for the company?

Following are some excellent sources of information on corporations:

Moody's Reports	800-342-5647
Standard and Poors	800-221-5277
Dun and Bradstreet	800-365-3867
Value Line Investment Survey	800-833-0046
Dow Jones Special Reports	800-445-9454
Fortune Magazine Special Reports	800-989-4636

You can order special reports on target companies. You'll have to pay for them, but if you're selective, the information will be a great adjunct to your research.

The key to finding out what you need to know is the most useful book I have in my office: Who's Who in America. *Who's in it? It seems damn near everybody, that's who.*

Harvey Mackay, *Swim with the Sharks*
Without Being Eaten Alive

Read the "Managing Your Career" column in *The Wall Street Journal* every Tuesday, and "You, Inc." by Marshall Loeb in each issue of *Fortune* magazine.

Check out *The Mission Statement Book* by Jeffery Abrahams or *A Sense of Mission* by Andrew Campbell and Laura L. Nash. Reading from these books will give you a good sense of how excellent companies define their values and their missions, which can help you evaluate target companies. Read the mission statements of your target companies, its competitors, and its key suppliers and customers before you go for that first interview.

Free one-stop career centers are springing up in larger communities as a result of alliances among state employment offices, community colleges and other related agencies. Check with your local private industry council or state social services or employment development department for the nearest one. Curtis A. Price went to the San Diego Center to take workshops that helped him prepare for starting his own business, including being referred for computer classes and entrepreneurial workshops.

Go to the library and read the last 12 or so issues of the *Journal of Career Planning and Employment.*

Whether you're currently searching for a job or not, subscribe to the *National Business Employment Weekly.* This weekly publication includes all classified employment advertisements from *The Wall Street Journal,* as well as excellent articles and information on career planning and job search (800-562-4868, $35 for eight weeks).

If you're interested in jobs outside the United States, subscribe to the *International Employment Gazette* (800-882-9188; 6 issues for $35.00). This publication lists 400-plus jobs every two weeks.

Also consider Canada; a three-issue subscription to *Canada Employment Weekly* is $15.00 (800-361-2580).

Check with your college career center. No matter how long ago you graduated, they can provide help. Many colleges have special programs for alumni.

Go for a drive. A taxi driver I met in Naples, Florida, was laid off from an industrial job (which he hated) in New Jersey. He and his wife hopped in the car and started driving. Six months later, as they drove into Naples, they both had the overwhelming feeling that they had found a home. He loves driving a cab, which lets him be outside and meet interesting people, and says he can't think of any single job that would lure him out of Naples.

If you're thinking about changing industries, trade shows are a great place to do research and networking. If you go to a trade show, prepare in advance. Find out who you want to see, and make arrangements to meet. Don't rely on luck. As you walk around the floor, don't get stuck spending too much time at one booth. Meet people, pick up as many handouts as you can carry and move along. Be respectful of the time of people you meet, especially if they're busy. If there's mutual interest, make an appointment to speak later. Pay attention. What are people wearing? What do they talk about? Is the general mood upbeat or downbeat? Are these people you would enjoy working with?

"You must have some idea of what it is you want to know." *That principle is so obvious it's embarrassing to even mention it. But I have met so many people who set out to do their information-gathering without the slightest idea of what they want*

*to know that it seems not only worth mentioning, but worth un-
derlining.*

Richard Nelson Bolles, *The Three Boxes of Life
and How to Get Out of Them*

Many trade shows have special programs for job seekers, including a place to leave your resume for prospective employers to review, and postings of available jobs. One way to learn about
trade shows is the publication *Trade Shows Worldwide* by Gale Research Inc., which is available in libraries.

Attend conferences. Phil Waltz, a 35-year-old chemical engineer in Cincinnati, earned a comfortable living as a factory
manager. But he was finding himself increasingly drawn to his
volunteer work, including taking inner-city children on outdoor
excursions. After attending a conference on natural resources and
environmental education, he resigned from his job and enrolled in
a graduate training program in natural resource management. Attending the conference was key, he told the *ReCareering Newsletter.* "I don't think I would have had the opportunity to talk to so
many environmental experts in any other setting."

Here are two newsletters that might help you in your career
planning and job search. Call and ask for a sample issue if
you're not sure about subscribing:

▶ *Kennedy's Career Strategist* (708-251-1661; monthly; $59 per
year).

▶ *ReCareering Newsletter* (708-735-1981; monthly; $59 per year).

I f you're considering an alternative type of career, or working on your own, order *The Whole Work Catalog* from The New Careers Center (303-447-1087). This catalog lists hundreds of books that can help you think about your career in a new way, and mount an effective job search campaign.

I f you're thinking of relocating, or you might be transferred by your company, order the publication "Relocation Guidance" from the *National Business Employment Weekly* (800-367-9600). It lists vital statistics, major employers and recruiters, and sources for obtaining local information.

R ead *Open Book Management* by John Case. If at all possible, go to work for a company that subscribes to the philosophies of open book management. When Charlotte Eckley left her job at Springfield Remanufacturing, one of the open-book pioneers, she asked to see the financial statements of her new company. The owner laughed at her. Nevertheless, over the next two years she convinced him to begin sharing more information and creating employee incentive packages for hitting financial targets. Within two years, sales had increased by 35 percent and employees had earned financial rewards.

F ind a company that offers equity or incentive pay in lieu of or in addition to the normal annual raise. Pay for performance and bonuses allow you to be recognized for your accomplishments, and are probably no less secure than jobs that have no performance incentives.

F ind out as much as you can about the person (or people) who had the job before you. Did the previous incumbent walk on water, meaning that no one could ever fill those shoes? Or has the job had a long string of short-termers, possibly suggesting that it's structured in a way that will assure your failure.

Read the classic motivational and self-help books, whether you feel like you need them or not, because eventually you'll interview with someone whose life has been changed as a result of reading something like: *How to Win Friends and Influence People* by Dale Carnegie; *The Power of Positive Thinking* by Norman Vincent Peele; or *Think and Grow Rich* by Napoleon Hill.

If you're very good and very tough, look for a turnaround opportunity. Patti Lewis left a career of senior positions at large corporations to become CEO of a failing doll company. It's been tough—she had to take the company through bankruptcy proceedings—but it's paying off. The company is now out of bankruptcy and profitable, and though recruiters are calling, she has no interest in leaving.

Wouldn't it be great if you could take a paid sabbatical? Here's one way to do it: write a book. Do enough research that you can prepare a proposal for a publisher (*How to Write a Book Proposal* by Michael Larsen is a good guide). Then submit it to publishers. If you write reasonably well, have selected a timely topic, and have a bit of luck, a publisher will finance your sabbatical with an advance. Then, you can finance the growth of your library by asking publishers for review copies of all the books you'll need to read. Getting the book published will do much to differentiate you from all the other job candidates in the world once you get serious with your job search. That is, assuming that your book doesn't sell so well that you decide to retire to the Caribbean instead.

Creativity is essential to success in a job search. Yet this attribute is an early casualty to the constant barrage of negative feedback. Creativity suffers when you lose the confidence to seek new ideas, the courage to implement them and the commitment to make them work. But without innovation in your job search, you're just another applicant.

Brian Jud, *Coping with Unemployment*

There are lots of excellent books available on career planning, career management and job search. Unfortunately, your library is unlikely to have most of them, and in many cases those that do will not be current. To see what's available, order catalogs directly from publishers or distributors that specialize in career books. The following list will give you a good start:

Bob Adams, Inc.	800-872-5627
Addison-Wesley Publishing	800-447-2226
Impact Publications	703-361-7300
JIST	800-648-5478
Kennedy Publications	800-531-0007
Ten Speed Press	800-841-2665
John Wiley & Sons, Inc.	800-225-5945
VGM Career Horizons	800-323-4900

Read lots of books on career planning and management. If you think you don't have time, at least read the Paradox 21 Special Reports *25 Books That Could Help Your Career, If Only You Had Time to Read Them.* You can order it by calling 800-644-3889.

One of the best books for getting you started on research regarding occupations, employers or industries is *Getting the*

Lowdown on Employers and a Leg Up on the Job Market by Leila K. Kight. This book is a wealth of research suggestions and specific recommendations concerning agencies and publications.

Spend an hour or so browsing the most current addition of *The Statistical Abstract of the United States.* Try to do it without any preconceived notions; if you're open-minded, lots of great ideas are going to jump out at you regarding your career or your business.

The following government agencies can be great sources of information:

International Trade Administration (ITA) has analysts who track domestic and foreign industries and markets (202-482-3808).

Bureau of the Census has industry specialists who can provide raw census data (301-763-4100).

International Trade Commission (ITC) studies unfair trade worldwide, and has data on specific companies (202-205-1819).

The Federal Trade Commission (FTC) studies competition between companies and the effect on industry as a whole (202-326-2222).

Go to your local library and ask for an online index to articles concerning the company or the industry in which you're interested.

Find the names of the key reporters and stock analysts who cover the industries and companies in which you're interested, and call them. Many will be willing to share their insights with you. This could be the best conceivable source of information to help you prepare for interviews.

Check with all trade associations in which the individuals or organizations you're researching might be members. Check your library for the *Encyclopedia of Associations* and the *National Trade and Professional Associations of the United States* catalogs.

If the company in which you're interested has been organized by one or more labor unions, call their headquarters and see what you can find out about the company from their perspective.

Many industries maintain lobbying offices in Washington, DC. This can be a great source of information concerning which leaders in that industry perceive to be the key national issues it faces.

Especially if you're interested in a smaller company or a local unit of a larger corporation, a local or state chamber of commerce or private industry council can be a great source of information.

Find out which university professors have done research in the industries or companies in which you're interested and try to schedule a telephone interview. Many business schools, for example, have scholarly publications including *Harvard Business Review* and *Sloan Management Review.*

If you're especially impressed by a particular career book, see if you can't schedule a telephone interview with the author for a personal consultation. Show your appreciation by recommending his or her book to all your friends.

Think futuristically. Try to anticipate what technology will do to your industry over the long term. Try to anticipate potential unseen competitors. To kick-start your futuristic thinking, contact the World Future Society in Washington, DC at 301-656-8274.

Whenever you call somebody for an informational interview:

▶ Know what you want.

▶ Be specific in your questions.

▶ Be efficient and respectful of the interviewee's time.

▶ Pay attention, be flexible, and prepared to let the conversation go in unexpected directions while still keeping a focus on the information that you require.

▶ Be polite and don't take more time than you promised.

▶ Take careful notes.

The *National Business Employment Weekly*'s premier guide, *Jobs Rated Almanac* by Les Krantz and Tony Lee, ranks 250 jobs according to income, environment, stress level, outlook, physical demands, security and other criteria. This is especially useful to someone beginning a career or contemplating a significant career change.

Nexis Express, a service of Nexis/Lexis, can send you a corporate profile on a target company including all business journal articles on the organization for a cost of $50 to $100. The number is 800-227-9597.

The best sources of information aren't in libraries, or even on the Internet. They are people actively out in the field who are familiar with what's happening *right now*. Make you ears do their part in the research effort; don't just rely on your eyes.

Online resources can be invaluable for job-search research. Christine Sullivan used online services extensively during her six-month job search. She says, "If you get a call from a headhunter at 4 in the afternoon for an interview at 9 the next morning, there's no other way you can get background information on the company."

One way of finding information about specific companies is to find their homepages on the World Wide Web.

The operational planning principle becomes that the ultrapreneur must get the facts, face the facts and act as the facts dictate—not as they used to act, or as others are acting, but as the facts now dictate.

James B. Arkbauer, *Ultrapreneuring: Taking a Venture from Start-Up to Harvest in Three Years or Less*

"Of course you understand that this is just a network meeting."

8

Networking

How would you like to have a web of friends, mentors and guardian angels all across the country—or the world? Think of networking as an investment in your personal worldwide web, not as a tool for landing your next job. Networking accounts for at least 60 percent of all successful job searches. It can even lead to a new job being created to match your qualifications. Paradoxically, a lifetime discipline of networking might be the single most important investment you'll ever make in your own job security. Not many employers want to lose someone who is well-connected.

Take advantage of the "six degrees of separation." This popular theory states that everyone in America is six or less handshakes away from everyone else.

Jay Levinson and Seth Godin,
The Guerrilla Marketing Handbook

D r. Sam Sackett, a vice president in the Oklahoma City office of Bernard Haldane Associates, a national retail outplacement consulting firm, says that getting a job is a lot easier if you hear about it early. Indeed, most hiring executives would like to avoid a national search if possible. For you, there's much less competition before a search starts. That's why Sackett recommends spending at least 30 hours every week on networking during a job search.

You would be hard-pressed to find a better networking role model than Gerald A. Michaelson. He wrote in a column in *Success* magazine that one should "never cease pushing the envelope to generate one more contact." Michaelson's phone directory is organized by city so that he can work local contacts with every flight. Prior to visiting a city, he books appointments for breakfast, lunch, dinner and drinks. While changing flights at a particular airport, he calls local contacts just to say hello. When possible, he takes advantage of domestic flight rules that allow a connection delay of up to four hours in order to book appointments during that window. "Never stop prospecting for intelligence," he says. "Be relentless. Ask everyone for information and opinions. You never know what unusual source will provide that critical idea that will catapult your business (or your job search) into the stratosphere."

Chuck Murphy stopped at the card table, curious as to why a street vendor would be selling books and T-shirts at the gathering point for a huge cross-country bike tour. The books, he learned, weren't for sale, but could be had only by making a charitable contribution to bike safety. He forked over his $10 and walked off with an autographed copy, having for the first time in his life left his business card with a street vendor. Several weeks later, he got a call at his printing business. It was the street vendor, wondering if Chuck would print a brochure. Chuck was happy to take the job, and even happier when he learned that the street vendor—who is actually only an amateur at street vending—did a significant amount of printing. The street vendor has been happy with the quality of Chuck's work. (But I'm still trying to get him to buy a "Never Fear, Never Quit" T-shirt.)

If you don't have a network yet, an online bulletin board is a fantastic place to start. Think about it—you have access to experts nationwide, all from your computer terminal.

Orville Pearson, Senior Vice President for Programs and
Professional Development, Lee Hecht Harrison Inc.

In the book *Networking,* which is one of the *National Business Employment Weekly*'s premiere employment guides, Douglas B. Richardson, president of his own career counseling and management development consulting firm in Bala Cynwyd, Pennsylvania, suggests capitalizing upon "Granfalloons" for your networking. Granfalloon is the term Kurt Vonnegut created in the novel *Cat's Cradle* for any group of people who seem to be related by some happenstance, such as being a golfer or a Tigers' fan.

"Being a member of a granfalloon gives you some interpersonal leverage with other members," Richardson says, allowing you to instantly create a more comfortable relationship. Richardson suggests using granfalloons in two ways. One, make a list of all granfalloons of which you're a member (for example, your alma mater) and start making calls. Two, find out all the granfalloons of which a networking contact is a member, so you can develop something in common to talk about other than the weather.

Brice Brausou was 60 years old when his executive vice president position with a national health care firm was eliminated. He'd been with the firm for 30 years, and negotiated a retirement package, though he wasn't ready to retire. In working with outplacement counselor Bruce McCroskey of The Innis Company in Dallas, it became clear that his knowledge of the health care industry, his extensive network of contacts and his enjoyment of working with people would make him an excellent health care recruiter. For this position, not only was his age not a detriment, it was an asset. He was able to select from several offers, finally accepting a position that guaranteed his old salary would be matched or exceeded, and allowed him to remain in Dallas.

Mark Carsman, an independent outplacement counselor in Montrose, New York, warns against confusing networking activity with results. He worked with one candidate whose networking, while extensive, had been singularly ineffective. After conducting a "pattern analysis," it was ascertained that there was no pattern of his choice of contacts. This lack of purpose carried through in his informational interviews, which were unfocused. Once the candidate clarified the desired work, his presentations became much more focused, and within several weeks he had two solid job offers.

One of the most effective ways to crash through the barriers erected to keep job seekers out is to have a current employee of the company carry your torch. Guy Kawasaki got his job at Apple Computer Co. because a college buddy carried his resume to human resources. Since Apple gets about 10,000 unsolicited resumes every month, Kawasaki probably never would have gotten the job without an inside contact.

Your ability to meet people, locate prospects, provide information and make sales depends entirely on your aggressiveness.

Jay Conrad Levinson and Charles Rubin,
*Guerrilla Marketing On Line: The Entrepreneur's
Guide to Earning Profits on the InterNet*

Things don't just "turn up" until you start turning over the rocks. Bob Adams lost a position of 28 years with a major telecommunications corporation. He'd worked with that company his entire adult life, and was given the opportunity to find a job internally that would allow him to complete another two years to receive his entire retirement package. He initiated a desultory telephone campaign, but it was a half-hearted effort because he assumed that something would turn up. When he found his calls not being returned, he joined a job-finders group, expanded his search effort and became more flexible in his expectations. He finally accepted a staff position in his old business unit.

J oe Meissner, president of Power Marketing, a San Francisco outplacement firm, gave the following advice in a *National Business Employment Weekly* article entitled "How to Work a Room": arrive early; eat quickly so you don't have to balance a plate; move constantly; don't hang out with friends; avoid alcohol; don't sit down at all; work your way into groups and introduce your way around; visit every vendor booth; get invited to hospitality suites; slip out of seminars before they start, and if you stay at a seminar, be sure to ask intelligent questions at the end; and exchange lots of business cards. You can take a nap on the plane flying home.

A ttend a Never Fear, Never Quit conference. This is the most cost-effective way to hear great success trainers and motivational speakers like Mark Victor Hansen and Thomas J. Winninger. It's also a superb opportunity for networking. For information call 800-644-3889.

O rder the videotape program, *Creative Job Search* by Brian Tracy from Nightingale-Conant (800-525-9000). Here's a great suggestion from that program: start your informational networking by doing a research project. Ask executives for 10 minutes to be interviewed, promising to share the results. Call back when you're done, but don't spill the beans over the phone! Get the executive's curiosity aroused. Then, when you share the results, you can also tell him or her why you've decided you want to work for that company, and what you could do for them.

Be aware of a simple truth: executive recruiters don't work for job hunters, they work for the companies that pay their fees, and that's where their loyalties will always lie.

Tony Lee, Editor, *National Business Employment Weekly*

Never try to turn an informational interview into a job interview. Warren Braun, president of Comsonics Inc., an electronics firm in Harrisonburg, Virginia, speaks for many in saying, "I can assure you that we wouldn't hire that individual if he [or she] were the last person on earth."

Warm up to cold calling. Think of it as making new friends. Recall the classic song from the early 1970s: "Reach out in the darkness and you may find a friend."

One job-search study found that people who networked with strangers made an average of $2,500 per year more than people who networked only with people they knew. Keep making new friends.

Susan Bard was a public relations professional with extensive health care experience seeking a media relations position with a hospital or other health care organization. She procured listings of local hospitals and the membership directory of a professional communications group. Then she started cold calling. She uncovered a newly formed position at a major hospital that had not yet been advertised, and got the job by beating the competition to the punch.

Donald Asher of Resume Righters in San Francisco, tells of a recent graduate with a degree in mechanical engineering. He was trying to find a job in Michigan at a time when the automobile industry was shrinking. He started in the A section of the yellow pages, and called every company to request an interview. For eight hours each day, he made cold calls. Within one week, he had appointments for 18 interviews. At a time when many other engineers were unemployed, the young man got a job in record time.

Be ready for an answering machine. Assume you'll reach voice-mail, and be ready to make a great impression. Convey an up-beat mood, and leave just enough of a message to make them want to speak with you. Don't ask for a callback. Instead, say when you'll be calling back, and make sure that you call exactly on time.

Don't try to sell yourself over the phone. The purpose of your call should be to schedule an interview so that you can sell yourself in person. Make the call as brief as possible, set the appointment, then hang up. Send a resume if you're asked to, but don't volunteer to; you're usually better off leaving it behind after having made a favorable impression in a face-to-face meeting.

Never assume that family or friends know of your situation, or that they aren't in a position to help. Stories abound of chance connections with a distant cousin, the garbage collector or a taxi driver resulting in the link to the perfect job.

Unfortunately, LUCK plays a starring role in what you accomplish through personal contacts. Who do you know? And does your inquiry come at the opportune time when someone you know happens to have, or know of, the right position?

John Lucht, *Rights of Passage at $100,000+*

Four months to the day after Blaine O'Connell left his job at Missouri Baptist Hospital in St. Louis, he called an old friend in North Carolina on a Thursday afternoon. The following day, the chief executive officer of Froedtert Hospital in Milwaukee called the same person, asking if she knew of potential candidates for a chief financial officer. That's the position that Blaine now holds.

Jeff Rinz was six months into the job he had always wanted when the company foundered, and he was laid off. During those six months, however, he had traveled extensively and given his business card—which mentioned his fluency in Spanish and Portuguese—to many people. He found another job, but after about three years that company also went under. At just about that time, he received a call from someone who had gotten his business card three years earlier about a position as a Latin American sales representative. Jeff jumped at the opportunity, which became the launching pad for his own business as an international broker of food service equipment. Many of his current clients are people with whom he made connections with in his earlier jobs. Jeff's philosophy is that to successfully grow one tree, you should plant 10 seeds.

Dr. Steven A. Schroeder was a professor of medicine at the University of California in San Francisco. He also developed a national reputation as a result of his work in health care policy. This visibility surfaced him as a candidate when the New Jersey-based Robert Wood Johnson Foundation—the nation's largest health philanthropy—was seeking a new president. Schroeder's national reputation, earned as a result of his optional activities, resulted in his getting the job.

Make at least two calls every day before 8 A.M.

Linda Barbanel, a New York psychotherapist, started giving free speeches about the psychology of money to promote her therapy practice. This led to magazine interviews about women and money and compulsive shopping. From there, she branched into speaking about children and money. One day, after a speech on the subject, she was approached by an agent about writing a book. The result was *Piggy Bank to Credit Card: Teaching Your Child the Financial Facts of Life.* When you start reaching out, you never know where it will take you.

Community service can reap unexpected rewards. Tom Cilek was a partner with a law firm in Iowa City, Iowa, between 1973 and 1986. He was also active in a wide variety of community projects. But it probably never would have occurred to him to apply for a job as the senior vice president of Hills Bank. While organizing a recognition for a farmer who had won a national plowing contest, he met Dwight Seegmiller, who was once national president of Future Farmers of America. Dwight became bank president a short time later. His first new hire would be Tom Cilek.

People who are willing to open their rolodex, pick up a phone, call on their contacts and ask for help, ideas and solutions, and who offer leads, information and ideas, are perceived as powerful and smart. The closest thing to knowing something is to know where and how to find it.

Susan RoAne, *The Secrets of Savvy Networking*

Another excellent networking source is joining professional associations. L. J. Nash, a records manager in Madison, Wisconsin, identified a company with excellent benefits and a good working environment, but was unsuccessful at getting a response via traditional methods. She went to a women's professional association regional meeting, and there met several managers from the company. This opened the door, and she eventually landed a job.

Mara Brown, author of *Landing on Your Feet: An Inspirational Guide to Surviving, Coping and Prospering from Job Loss,* suggests that you be careful about selecting the people with whom you network. Don't inadvertently throw around the name of somebody who has no credibility with peers, or let yourself be introduced by someone who is seen as a loser.

Executive recruiter Gary Knisely of New York-based Johnson Smith & Knisely Accord recommends calling at least 25 key competitors, suppliers, stock analysts, management consultants and former colleagues every three to six months in order to maintain your visibility. These will be the first people you would contact in a job search.

If you read lots of career books (which you should), you'll eventually come across the advice to not spend time on informational interviews with people who don't have hiring authority. This may, however, be shortsighted. People lacking hiring authority can be both an entree to somebody who does have such authority, and give you valuable inside information so that you're better prepared to ask intelligent questions during subsequent interviews.

Get out of the office. A data processing manager at a trucking company survived several downsizings, which he saw as a wake-up call to expand his networking with other professionals in the computer field. Although he's still with the trucking company, he says networking has enabled him to maintain more control over his career and reduced the fear of being victimized by circumstances beyond his control.

Become a customer of the companies with which you do informational interviewing. One job searcher purchased a watch made by a watch company with which he had an interview, and then made sure it was noticed.

When do you begin to put your flirting knowledge into practice?
Right now! Begin by taking the first step to reach out to others
. . . . Smile to the person you pass in the grocery store. Learn the
name of the person who answered the phone at the business you
just called, listen to the passenger who sits next to you on the
airplane.

Jill Spiegel, *Flirting for Success*

Paula Stanford, founder of Human Resources Network in Oklahoma City, suggests cultivating as many contacts as possible at the level to which you wish to report. If you want to be chief operating officer or chief financial officer, make friends with chief executive officers. If being CEO is your goal, get to know people who are on corporate boards of directors.

Peter Milner was determined to learn everything he could about companies he'd targeted for potential employment. He made a point of attending every public forum at which a company employee was speaking. One corporation—Beers Construction Company in Atlanta—impressed him because people at all levels of the organization were out giving speeches about the company. He now works there.

Joan Lloyd, a Milwaukee career professional with a syndicated newspaper column and television program, says that while it's possible to conduct effective networking while currently employed, you must avoid using company resources and abusing company time. It's essential, she says, to have a system. Set your networking goals at the beginning of the week, and use every morning, noon and evening for networking. Couple your networking with professional meetings wherever possible. Also, be realistic about the likelihood that as your networking efforts expand, word may eventually come back to your organization.

William J. Morin, formerly chairman of Drake, Beam, Morin Inc. in New York, describes what can happen when someone begins aggressive networking without a plan. A human resources executive lost a job in a companywide cutback. She immediately began networking with the many people she knew, but didn't spend time defining her goals and unique selling proposition. She packed her calendar with informational interviews, and her networking soon became "a helter-skelter activity, and not an organized and integral part of an overall job search," Morin says.

The candidate should have focused on key targets rather than seeing anyone who would agree to meet with her; been more direct when asking about existing openings and the identity of hiring authorities; and made more effective use of the telephone, rather than having lots of face-to-face meetings with people who couldn't really help her.

Networking letters should be short, to the point and personalized. They shouldn't include a resume, since this makes you look over-anxious and puts the contact person in an uncomfortable position.

Every networking contact you make, even those by telephone, should be followed by a prompt thank-you note.

Ariella Ginoza was having no luck in her efforts to pursue a career in human resources. A mentor advised her to become active in human resources professional organizations. She began regularly attending association meetings, and eventually met a recruiter who helped her land a job in the field.

Forty Plus is an organization of professional men and women over the age of 40 who are looking for jobs. There are 20 chapters in large cities around the country. You must apply and submit accept-able references and pay a fee to join. The organization has no em-ployees, and expects each member to volunteer two days per month of service. The organization provides computer resources, a li-brary, a weekly strategy group, emotional support and other re-sources. To find the one nearest you, call the New York office at 212-233-6086.

Identifying the potential benefits of a meeting, party, convention or whatever is one of the best ways to motivate, tantalize or prod ourselves into making the most of each event. It builds purpose and confidence, and that leads to even more confidence.

Susan RoAne, *How to Work a Room*

If you're an executive and willing to relocate, consider joining one or more of the following job search networks:

Exec-U-Net	203-851-5180
The Search Bulletin	703-759-4900
Net Share Inc.	415-883-1700
Human Resources Network	616-837-7857
CEO Update	202-408-7900
Executive Edge	800-546-3343

You'll go through a period of time when, despite all the mail you're sending out and the phone calls you're making, your phone doesn't ring. Just remember that Winston Churchill once said that anyone destined to accomplish great things must first spend time alone in the desert. This is the time when you're preparing yourself intellectually and emotionally for the great things to come.

One of the best books on networking is Jill Spiegel's *Flirting for Success*. Don't be put off by the title; Spiegel defines flirting as "building your self-esteem and the self-esteem in others by creating a warm, honest and sincere rapport." You can be a success, Spiegel says, "if you believe in yourself, appeal to people as kind human beings instead of preconceived stereotypes and make sincere contact with others." Her book is filled with excellent practical advice on how to do exactly that.

Create a diverse community of friends and supporters to stand by you during your job search.

Be involved in networking, not notworking. Know what you're after, be efficient and don't delude yourself into thinking that pleasant conversations are getting you any closer to a job offer.

Judy Anderson, founder of a Farmingdale, New York, consulting firm that bears her name, suggests doing job-search networking on the golf course, since so many business executives love to play golf. This will also give you something to talk about in your interviews, and a skill that could help you later in your career.

An effective networking meeting has a predetermined purpose, a structure and an agenda. Slipping your resume under someone's vodka gimlet doesn't qualify.

Douglas B. Richardson, *Networking*

Start a personal newsletter and send it to members of your mailing list, perhaps on a quarterly basis. Include in it your personal news, ideas and thoughts. Solicit contributions from others (editorial, not financial). This can be a highly efficient form of networking, and if you keep it going and make it interesting, people will look forward to it.

Read as much as you can before any informational interview. You cannot tire out books or magazine articles with dumb questions.

Paul Hawkinson publishes the *Fordyce Letter* for the executive search industry, but still spends several weeks every year "in the trenches" working with a search firm. He says he has less trouble getting in to speak with corporate CEOs than he does "HR grunts." The latter, he says, "have rotten jobs—the only people they have power over is the poor job hunter." He says the best time to reach CEOs is at 7:30 A.M. or 6:00 P.M. When he calls, he says only: "Do you have a moment for just one question? Of all the top executive functions reporting directly to you, which would you categorize as currently being less than 100 percent effective?" This question frequently results in his snagging an assignment to conduct a search. Modify his approach, and you may well snag a job.

Make telephone calls to your peers at other companies. Everyone is afraid of losing jobs in corporate restructuring, and most people will want to cooperate with you now in hopes that you may be able to help them in the future.

Send congratulatory notes to people you read about in the newspaper who have received promotions, won awards or been given other honors.

Never make cold calls on a Monday morning or a Friday afternoon.

If you're working with a recruiter, make sure he or she knows whether your resume is posted on any computerized database, or whether you're working with another recruiter. If a company independently finds your name on a database while it's submitted by a recruiter, or if two recruiters simultaneously submit your name for the same job, there's likely to be a fight over payment of a fee. The probable outcome is that you become more trouble than you're worth to either party, and are dropped as a candidate.

Joining organizations and taking time to network is an investment no different than buying office equipment or creating a marketing piece. You're negligent if you don't focus on achieving the maximum return from that investment.

Alan Weiss, *Million Dollar Consulting*

WORKING WITH RECRUITERS

Use these guidelines when working with executive recruiters:

1. View it as a two-way relationship.

2. Expect to help them as much as you hope they'll help you.

3. Tell recruiters the truth about your background and abilities.

4. Don't waste their time on the telephone.

5. Take their advice seriously.

6. It's okay to work with more than one at a time, but let each know who else you're working with.

7. If you're not interested in a position that's available, try to help the recruiter identify other appropriate candidates who might be.

8. Never express interest in a job if you're not genuinely interested.

9. Express your thanks for any help provided.

If you anticipate working with executive recruiters, the book *Rites of Passage at $100,000+* by John Lucht should be on your "must" reading list.

Contact Kennedy Publications (603-585-3001) to obtain *The Directory of Executive Recruiters,* which is available in book, on PC disk and label format. Another helpful publication is *Kennedy's Pocket Guide to Working with Executive Recruiters.* From that volume, here's some good advice from Don Baiocchi, a Chicago outplacement and management consultant: "Unless you've got significant geographic preferences or restrictions, and perhaps even if you do, you should send a cover letter and a resume to the entire 1,000+ list of retained executive search firms and each of their offices. This will maximize the chance of getting your resume into their retrieval system." Follow up with personal letters to each search consultant you personally know.

If you're called by a recruiter, and have never heard of his or her firm, promise to get back to him or her and check out the firm before you do. A good place to start is by contacting the Association of Executive Search Consultants in New York City at 212-949-9556, which is the professional association for search firms.

Never let any search firm send out your resume without your specific approval, and never send a resume to a search firm—especially a contingency search firm—without specific instructions that it's not to be sent to anyone without your approval on each prospective job.

Have a prepared script that summarizes your qualifications, interests and accomplishments in case a recruiter calls. You'll have about two minutes; don't stumble and fumble.

Until you actually have a job, one of your chief goals each week should be to add people to your network. How many you add is up to you, but if you aren't having success drumming up leads, 10 new network leads per week does not seem to me to be an unreasonable goal.

Max Messmer, *50 Ways to Get Hired*

ELECTRONIC NETWORKING

Use technology to get your rolodex in shape. Time management expert Jeffrey J. Mayer studied more than two dozen different personal information manager computer programs, and decided that ACT! by Symantec was by far the best. His book *ACT! for Dummies* describes in detail how this system can be used to organize your rolodex and your calendar. You can order a demonstration disk from the company by calling 800-441-7234. The program can be mail-ordered from Computer City Direct for $179.97 by calling 800-843-2489.

If you do elect to utilize ACT!, following are several ancillary products that can make it more efficient:

The HP 200 LX palm top computer by Hewlett-Packard ($625 for 1 MB; $825 for 2 MB) is preloaded with ACT!, including a transfer cable. With 1 MB, it holds up to 1,000 contacts, and can be upgraded with memory cards to a total of 40 MB (Real Estate Computer Solutions, Inc.; 800-962-9651).

Use Card Scan to input business cards into ACT!. This program automatically enters the card text into appropriate categories and retains an image of the original card. The cost is $249, or $99 if used with your existing scanner (Corex, 800-942-6739).

The *Easy ACT!* newsletter from Pinnacle Publishing is $79 for 12 monthly issues, with the first issue free. This gives suggestions for making more effective use of the computer program, and can be obtained by calling 800-788-1900.

If a sophisticated program like ACT! or similar programs (including Sharkware by Cognitec at $130, ECCO-PRO by Net-Manage, $99; or Desk-Top Set by Okna Corp., $199) is more than you need, consider getting Sidekick by Starfish Software for about $50. According to *Fortune* magazine writer Stratford Sherman, who evaluated available programs, this one is probably "best suited to the needs of most users—attractive, efficient easy to use."

Warning! Just buying ACT!, with or without accessories, or any other personal information manager, will not turn you into a networking or time-management wizard. It's just a tool, and you must learn how to use it to support effective networking habits.

Robert Coffey spent 13 months on his job search. He set up his own electronic database management system for all of his contacts, and set up customized reports. This let him know that 11 percent of his responses to ads, 6 percent of his recruiter contacts and 4 percent of his networking contacts resulted in interviews. This realization prompted him to spend more time customizing cover letters, resumes and addenda to the requirements of every classified advertisement to which he responded. Though he now has a job, he continues to maintain his database.

Never ask for a job; always ask for suggestions. Don't ask for favors; ask for advice.

William Morin and James Cabrera, *Parting Company*

A simple tape recorder, available from Radio Shack or other such outlet, can help you improve your networking by telephone. Simply tape record several phone calls and compare your actual performance with your preestablished expectations.

No matter how old you are, no matter what you do, if you're not comfortable with a computer, this would be a great time to stop surfing the channels and start surfing the Net. Linda Klein, a principle with the Arbor Group in New York City, tells of the managing director of an investment bank who is in his mid-50s and has been with the company for more than 20 years. His concern at being unable to compete with younger people prompted him to sign up for an evening course to learn how to do word processing. The training, he says, has helped boost his self-confidence, and he appreciates that it's not as difficult as he feared it would be.

Stephanie Hammonds, a computer graphics instructor with the Veteran's Technical Training Program at the Vietnam Veteran's Workshop in Boston, describes the following 12 ways to enhance your technical skills without spending a lot of money:

1. Take classes at a local high school or adult education center.

2. Get involved with professional and industry associations.

3. Find organizations that provide special discounts to people who are unemployed.

4. Get a book and study on your own.

5. Use online tutorials.

6. If you don't have a PC and can't afford to buy one, lease one for a time.

7. Hang around at computer retail stores speaking with clerks.

8. Exchange a service you can provide to someone else who can tutor you about computers.

9. Check to see whether your local unemployment office or area nonprofit agencies provide training.

10. Join a computer group or society.

11. Watch the newspaper for ads for free or low-cost workshops.

12. Take every possible class you can at the job.

The future is here, and it's online. There's a world of information and opportunity available through commercial services, the Internet and its World Wide Web. The chapter on career planning includes specific recommendations on getting yourself hooked up. Once you're online, electronic mail, bulletin board services and discussion groups will provide you with a powerful source of networking. Electronic networking is highly efficient, and provides you an opportunity to link up with many people who are very well-connected themselves.

Karen Kay wanted to switch careers and become a technical writer. She got her first few leads by getting onto the Internet, and got connected with hundreds of people worldwide. This gave her multiple tips and job leads. The computer allowed her to have "conversations" with hundreds of people at a time, and to launch her business.

Put your e-mail address on your business card.

Whether you've met the corporate ax or just feel antsy about your career, the online possibilities are getting too big to ignore.

Marshall Loeb, *Fortune*

"Oh, hi . . . just pull up a pile of resumes and have a seat."

9

Resumes and Cover Letters

If you're lucky, your resume will receive a 30- to 40-second scan on the first pass. Even then, the reader will be looking for reasons to exclude—rather than include—you from consideration. Use your resume to summarize accomplishments rather than experiences, and to convey a sense of your enthusiastic, can-do personality. Don't stray far beyond traditional conventions most employers expect to see, and make it easy for them to trust you (for example, by not leaving any unexplained gaps in your chronology) and like you (by conveying the sense that you take initiative). Develop a different resume for electronic job searching that emphasizes the key words software programs look for.

When you tailor your core resume to fit a specific job, you pay the employer the ultimate compliment. Even when the employer recognizes your customized resume as pure strategy, the employer will like it and will like you. Nobody doesn't like being singled out for attention.

Joyce Lain Kennedy and Thomas J. Morrow,
Electronic Resume Revolution

Bob Patton wanted to make a change. For five years, he'd been the administrator of a large clinical department in a teaching hospital. But it was clear to him that he'd enjoy a more rewarding career managing a medical group practice. After fruitless months of sending resumes summarizing his significant achievements at the hospital, Patton finally did some market research: he called the places where he'd been rejected and asked why.

Time after time he heard the same: not enough managed-care experience. He redid his resume and cover letter to focus on group practice needs rather than on his own proudest accomplishments. He even prepared a supplemental sheet on his managed-care work. Within months, he was flying across the country for interviews, and shortly thereafter accepted the ideal job.

Some job-search guides suggest conducting a search without a resume. It's true that a resume in itself is an ineffective job-search tool, as Richard Bolles points out in *What Color Is Your Parachute?* The fact is, however, that the resume is such an accepted part of the job-search scene that you must have one. Like wearing the right suit of clothes, a resume might not get you the job, but it's necessary to get you through the front door.

Keep your resume current. When someone (for example, a recruiter) asks you for a resume, he or she doesn't mean next week. If you don't have one ready, the recruiter may move on to someone else. The process of keeping it updated can also help you analyze your career progress and be prepared for performance reviews.

Some career experts admonish you to keep your resume to one or, at most, two pages at all costs, while others consider this an unnecessary straightjacket. The best advice is probably provided by Max Messmer, chairman of Robert Half International, who advises using a second page to describe important aspects of your background, but only if the information is relevant to the specific job search.

I recommend having two versions of your resume: an electronic resume to help you attract the attention of the robotic recruiter, and a traditional paper copy to assist in selling yourself in face-to-face real-people situations.

John D. Erdlen, Executive Director,
Northeast Human Resources Association

The single greatest difference between effective and ineffective resumes is that ineffective resumes describe duties and responsibilities, but provide no sense of the person behind the paper. Effective resumes describe accomplishments and convey the picture of someone who is energetic, enthusiastic and capable. A simple formula for conveying this image is to use *action verbs* and *numbers* to describe and quantify your accomplishments. (This formula doesn't apply to electronic resumes, as we will see.)

Read Robert Half's *Resumania* column in the last issue of the *National Business Employment Weekly* each month. It will give you some good laughs and great resume pointers. But try to keep your own resume out of it!

Write your resume yourself. Don't turn it over to an outplacement or career counselor or a resume writing service. Even if you seek advice, do the writing yourself. Adhering to someone else's cookie cutter format is less powerful than telling your story.

Read the *National Business Employment Weekly's Premier Guide to Resumes* by Taunee Besson, president of Career Dimensions, a Dallas career consulting firm. In particular, the 11-page "Functional and Transferable Skills Inventory" will help you with both self-assessment and resume preparation. This book also contains many examples of effective resumes.

If you need help writing your resume, look for someone who has been certified by the Professional Association of Resume Writers. To be referred to the firm nearest you, call 800-677-9090.

You . . . can't really afford to ignore the changes in resume formatting and distribution [being created by online posting], because the impetus for the switch to the electric format has come from employers.

Pam Dixon and Sylvia Tiersten,
Be Your Own Headhunter On-Line

Take the Michelangelo approach to sculpting your resume. At the first stage, you're just making rough cuts. Don't worry about how it looks, and include everything you can think of. At this stage, it's okay if your resume is 50 pages long. Next comes the forming stage. Here's where you do your cutting and editing, hopefully with feedback from others you trust. Finally comes the polishing stage. This is where you refine it down to one or two pages, give it the graphic look you want and tailor it for individual opportunities.

Charles Logue, author of the book *Outplace Yourself: Secrets of an Executive Outplacement Counselor,* suggests using a portfolio as a companion piece to the resume. It should, however, be used discreetly, perhaps only after the first interview when things seem to be getting serious. The portfolio might include a table of contents, a personal summary, career overview, summaries of projects and major accomplishments, educational information associations and references.

Rick Oakton was president of his own industrial and commercial building development and investment company in Orange County, California. After 13 years, however, his business was having serious financial difficulties, and Oakton decided to seek employment with a larger development company. He worked with Career Strategy Associates of Newport Beach, California, to develop a "Career Transition Portfolio," which was a handsome leather zippered case including a resume, listings of major strategic alliances and joint ventures and brochures. The impressive presentation—always delivered via Federal Express—got Oakton the job he wanted.

If you list a Web resume address that people can look at for more information, potential employers can get a much better feel for the real you.

Pam Dixon and Sylvia Tiersten,
Be Your Own Headhunter On-Line

Keep in mind what prospective employers will be looking for from your resume:

1. An accounting of where you've been since graduating from school.

2. How your education and experience will help the company solve its problems and increase its profits.

3. A record of your meaningful accomplishments, and evidence that promises significant future contributions to the organization.

4. A sense of what kind of person you are.

It's no longer necessary to have your resume typeset, but it should be laser-printed on high-quality paper. With laser printers now available for less than $500, this is a good investment if you don't already have ready access to one, so that you can quickly customize resumes for each opportunity.

S ending a specially tailored resume for each job opportunity will do much to sell your credentials to prospective employers. It's important, however, that you keep track of who received which version of your resume.

T here are four basic resume styles:

1. Chronological (starting with the most current job and working backwards, listing jobs you've held and accomplishments at each).

2. Functional (which doesn't include a job history, but lists your accomplishments under such functional headings as finance or marketing).

3. Hybrid (a functional resume that also has a job history).

4. Curriculum vitae (mainly used in academic settings).

Generally, human resource people who screen resumes prefer the chronological format. But whichever you use, don't leave any unexplained time gaps. Since the reader will spend only 30 seconds or so with your resume, don't give him or her any reasons to suspect you have a troubled past.

Any employer will hire any applicant so long as he or she is convinced that it will bring more value than it will cost.

Tom Jackson, *Guerrilla Tactics in the New Job Market*

When building your resume (and career), keep in mind that the greatest strength is often a combination of strengths. Dr. Mike Magee was a skilled urologist who also found that he had a knack for administration. He began to study and become more involved in hospital management, eventually becoming a full-time executive. He also pursued his interests in medical communications by writing extensively and developing his own television program. With this matrix of skills, Dr. Magee has options not available to most surgeons. He currently is senior vice president at The Pennsylvania Hospital and professor of surgery at Jefferson Medical College in Philadelphia.

Remember that, although it's your resume, in the eyes of readers it's not really about you. What they're hoping to see is a mirror that reflects their own organizational values, culture and aspirations.

If you're unemployed and anticipate that it might be many months before you land a job, consider starting a business. In the long run, this may look better than having a black hole on your resume. If you do start a business, however, make sure you've got something to show that it was real, such as a brochure, customer list or product.

If you do decide to start a business, your business plan research can also be an effective means of job hunting. An executive who wouldn't take a call from a job hunter might well speak with you about your ideas for new products or services that could help his or her business. The conversation could, of course, always get around to the possibility of you developing your business as an associate of the company.

Another way of avoiding black holes on your resume is through temporary work. Temping opportunities have never been better, especially if you'd like to learn new skills. Even senior-level folks are working as temps these days.

An assignment abroad, once thought to be a career dead-end, has become the ticket to speedy advance.

Marshall Loeb, *Fortune*

Seek copies of resumes from people in jobs like the one you'd like to have, including people to whom you'd report, peers and job-search competitors. One way to gather resumes is to call and congratulate people who got jobs for which you'd applied unsuccessfully, and ask them to share their resume so you can learn more about strengthening your own.

If you need help writing your resume, look for someone who's been certified by the Professional Association of Resume Writers. For a referral to a firm near you, call 800-677-9090.

Many organizations have implemented 360-degree assessment programs affording every employee the chance to be evaluated by superiors, subordinates and peers. Do a 360 on your resume. Ask former supervisors, peers and subordinates to critique it for you.

Brenda Barrett had been director of operations for her family's insurance business, but wanted to move into the nonprofit world. She developed a functional resume that emphasized her transferable skills, and tailored it for each prospect, highlighting the skills and accomplishments most applicable to the desired job. By showing how her professional and volunteer experience was appropriate, she secured a job as volunteer director for the Dallas Hospice Center Inc.

The problem with most resumes, even if they are carefully prepared, is that they end up listing employment, position and responsibilities without ever indicating the potential value of the resume writer to the new employer.

Robert Half, *How to Get a Better Job in This Crazy World*

Here are 10 things not to include in your resume:

1. Your photograph.

2. References or even a statement that references are available (of course they are!).

3. Any information that it would be illegal for an employer to ask (race, age, disabilities and so on).

4. Salary history or expectations.

5. Personal or family information.

6. The title of every seminar you've ever attended or paper you've published.

7. Political interests and activities.

8. Reason for leaving the last job.

9. Humor.

10. The pronoun "I".

While you should generally exclude hobbies and outside interests, some experts say there are exceptions. For example, if you run marathons, this may be a plus for certain hiring executives. Of course, they may expect you to work marathon hours on the new job.

Construct a resume that portrays you as a generalist with specialized skills, not as a specialist. The world is changing too fast for you to pigeonhole yourself.

Show me a person who can't distill a lifetime onto two pages and I'll show you a scatterbrain or an egomaniac.
James Kennedy, Publisher, Directory of Executive Recruiters

Think about how your resume will look four to five years from now. Keep a 3×5 card file box and keep in it accomplishments that could be used for future resume updates. Whenever possible, include numbers, names of others who helped with the accomplishment and other appropriate information. Periodically, look through your card file box for obvious gaps, which can be used to guide you in seeking new project assignments.

Keep your old calendars for at least five years. They may come in handy if you need to go back and reconstruct your work history or accomplishments.

If you have computer skills, include a reference to them on your resume. If you don't, you'd better get them.

One of the most difficult obstacles to overcome in making the transition to a new industry is convincing potential employers that your skills truly are transferable. One way is write several short (one-page) case studies showing how you solved significant problems or achieved important goals in previous jobs. Use these headings:

▶ The nature of the challenge.

▶ What I did.

▶ Outcomes.

▶ Lessons learned.

From your research, you'll know the target company's most pressing problems. Write the case study to showcase how you've solved similar problems in a different setting.

Writing a great resume is a lot like painting a house. Before you apply the paint, you have to buy the right materials, assemble them and prepare your surface. If you neglect these initial steps, your final product will probably fall short of your standards.

Taunee Besson, *National Business Employment Weekly's Premier Guide to Resumes*

Pay attention to graphic design. The fonts you choose, the way you lay out information on the page and even the quality of paper you select will say a lot about you. Dorothy Hazzard, a resume professional in Honolulu, Hawaii, says most people are too conservative. If, she says, staid old Harvard University uses crimson printing on gray paper, and adding a second color in advertising increases readership, you might want to consider spiffing up your resume with a touch of color.

Differentiate yourself in delivery. Instead of mailing a resume, send it by courier or Federal Express or even hand deliver it yourself wearing your best suit. *Do not* hire the Whacky Balloon Lady to drop it off.

Think of your telephone and resume as conjoined twins. Before sending out a resume, try to speak with someone on the telephone first, and never send a resume without a follow-up phone call.

Try to avoid sending a resume by mail if at all possible. It's better left in person after an interview. If someone asks for a resume over the phone, see if you can forestall its delivery by ticking off your key attributes.

Resumes are the common currency of the job market. For this reason alone, I am against job-search guides that encourage you to avoid using a resume. Employees are suspicious of candidates who withhold their resumes.

Donald Asher, *The Overnight Job Change Strategy*

Dennis Sullivan, a career counselor at the Montgomery County Private Industry Council in Manasses, Virginia, describes how giving punch to the first line in a resume can result in a successful job search. He worked with one young woman with outstanding organizational abilities, and they came up with the line "Creates order out of chaos" to begin the professional summary section of her resume. Within several weeks, she had a number of interviews—always with companies where the office was a mess.

Put your resume on your business card. When Maggie Tinsman was running for the U.S. Senate in Iowa, on the back of her business card she listed her accomplishments under the heading "A Record of Leadership."

For a resume/business card that really makes an impression, contact Dave Bruno & Associates at 800-870-4410. Bruno is producer of *Success Gold Cards,* which have sold more than one million copies. For a reasonable price, Bruno can give you a business card that has the heft and feel of a top-quality credit card.

COVER LETTERS

Always make sure that your cover letter conveys that you've studied the target company and understand its problems.

Taunee Besson, in her book *Cover Letters,* one of the *National Business Employment Weekly*'s Premier Guides, says that all good cover letters should include:

1. Why you're specifically interested in that potential employer.

2. Why that employer should be interested in you (you were referred by a familiar person, your experience fits a current need, you've got a particularly strong background and so on).

3. When and how you'll be contacting the addressee to follow up and schedule an appointment.

She says you should use research and networking to find out what to include in your cover letter and to whom it should be addressed. The book features lots of "before and after" examples.

Ten things to leave out of your cover letter: humor, anger, greed, demands, lies, whining, presumptions, grandiose language, ego, grammatical or spelling errors.

Donald Asher, author of *The Overnight Job Change Strategy,* has this great idea: When you send a letter to a hiring authority, accompany it with a personalized note to that person's secretary explaining why it should be given directly to the boss, rather than being shunted to human resources.

In researching for this book, I read every cover letter book I could find. In the best of them, I found advice that I thought was horrible. In the worst of them, I found worthwhile advice. What's the point? A cover letter should be a reflection of you. Read books, speak with others and look at examples, but in the end, you must use your own judgment and write a cover letter that conveys your wonderful qualities and enthusiasm, and which will make it through the defenses the target company have erected to screen candidates out.

To give yourself the best chance of surviving the cover-letter purging process, your letter must entice an interviewer to get to know you better. Tell her why you've chosen her company over the many others that might employ you. Impress her with your desire to discuss the exciting possibilities waiting for you at her firm. Make her feel special. People respond to positive feedback, even (maybe even especially) when they're plowing through a boring stack of cover letters.

Taunee Besson, *National Business Employment Weekly's Premier Guide to Cover Letters*

Here's one way to be more flexible in your cover letter. Instead of simply applying for a job, hold forth the possibility of working as a consultant or on a temporary basis. An employer who might not want to hire you full-time may well want to try you out temporarily.

Here are some rules of direct mail that can be effectively used in your own direct-mail job-search campaign. Effective solicitations are always framed in terms of benefits to the customer, not selling a product that the vendor thinks is wonderful. They always define a unique selling proposition, that combination of benefits that makes this particular offering better than the competition. The message is always straightforward and easy to understand, and not clouded by unnecessary words or abstract arguments. They have the feel of a personal letter. Even though you know it's a mass mailing, you feel as though the writer really is speaking to you. The letter virtually compels you to at least scan the enclosures. The offering has punch, both because of the story it tells, the creative use of language and a graphically appealing layout.

All good direct mail includes a P.S. Your cover letter should, too; reiterate the single strongest reason why the addressee should invite you for an interview.

Never fax a resume, especially an unsolicited resume, unless you've been requested to do so. Be first class and send it first class.

*N*ever send a resume without a cover letter.

I look for a document that will tell me in one or two pages what specific business or professional experience a candidate has had, what the candidate has accomplished in his or her career and what sort of training and education the person has had.

Max Messmer, *50 Ways to Get Hired*

Don't send a resume to a post office box without first having tried to discover the name of the company and hiring executive. A bit of snooping can help not only land your resume on the right desk, it'll also display the level of resourcefulness and initiative many employers are looking for.

If you're working with an outplacement firm, make deliberate changes from their standard resume and cover letter format to avoid inadvertently stamping your work with an outplacement firm's "signature."

Have fun writing an Outrageous Resume that highlights all of your flaws, foibles and failings. Keep it in a safe place so that you never send it to a prospective employer by mistake!

Developing an overly broad career objective probably isn't helpful. If you have one, make sure it's focused. For example, write "brand management for consumer products," rather than "an opportunity to use my marketing skills."

If you use a summary paragraph rather than an objective statement, use it as an opportunity to come across as a real person— a sort of mini-cover letter, which summarizes your qualifications, capabilities and aspirations.

Some career experts will advise you to limit your resume to one page or two at the most, while others downplay this imperative if you're highly experienced or qualified. Try this: write a long one and a short one, then use your judgment with each opportunity as to which one to use.

Write the letter as if you were talking to someone. Keep it natural, and use your own language. Remember: letters reflect you and your style.

Charles H. Logue, *Outplace Yourself: Secrets of an Executive Outplacement Counselor*

ELECTRONIC RESUMES

Electronic resumes follow very different rules from paper resumes. With a paper resume, action verbs dominate, and you should avoid jargon and buzzwords. In electronic resumes, nouns dominate, while buzzwords and keywords are essential. It's reasonably safe to send multiple different resumes in paper version; electronic versions can be compared and cause problems. In paper resumes, graphic appeal is important, while a no-frills style is better electronically. And paper resumes should be one or two pages, while electronic resumes are more forgiving on length.

Before sending an electronic resume via e-mail or posting it on a resume database, surf the Net for a while (only after you've read a good book on the subject, such as *Finding a Job on the Internet* (McGraw-Hill) by Alfred Glossbrenner). Get a feel for what other people's electronic resumes look like; figure out the most important keywords to include; use lots of synonyms to optimize your chances of "a hit" in any given search; and construct a resume that's sufficiently precise to catch the computer's attention, and sufficiently interesting to catch a human reader's eye.

10
Interviewing

Prepare for every interview as though it's the most important sales call you'll ever make. Learn as much as you can about the company and the people you'll be meeting; anticipate the questions you'll be asked; create responses that are succinct and information-filled; and prepare yourself mentally and emotionally to be alert and enthusiastic. Begin each interview by finding out expectations for the person who's hired, and make sure you keep conversations focused on how and why you can meet them. Watch the interviewer's body language and expressions for clues on how to tailor your approach.

All the world's a stage, and never more so than during a job interview. Your goal during every interview is to bring the audience to its feet. Make sure that you're well-rehearsed, properly outfitted and emotionally prepared.

Good questions help you determine whether you have the skills and qualifications to do the job, illuminate which areas of your experience to showcase and build interview rapport. Bad questions, on the other hand, can drive a wedge between you and the interviewer.

Arlene S. Hirsch, Interviewing

How you manage the interview process can be the difference between landing a job and collecting another rejection letter. Ray Cech, president of Dunhill Executive Search in Los Angeles, tells of one candidate who was applying for the position of global director of health and safety at a large computer company. At the end of a day full of interviews, the candidate requested 15 minutes to make a presentation on what he'd do if offered the job. He was given a flip chart and an hour with the staff. Because of his research, he was able to give an outstanding presentation—and got the job.

Paul Ivey, in his book *Successful Salesmanship,* says that the personality of a successful salesperson must include enthusiasm, sincerity, tact and courtesy. An interview is a sales pitch, so the morning of any interview, remind yourself of how enthusiastic, sincere, tactful and courteous you are.

During an interview, look outward, not inward. Pay more attention to the needs and opportunities at the company than to your own desires and accomplishments, and you'll make a better impression.

Joseph A. Burns, an outplacement counselor with Lee Hecht Harrison Inc. in Ho-Ho-Kus, New Jersey, describes an interviewing danger that must be avoided by people with extensive technical knowledge. A 20-year engineering veteran with a large computer manufacturing company had his position eliminated in a general downsizing. He was very discouraged as he remembered a past job search in which he'd had 18 interviews without an offer.

In practice interviews, the problem became evident: he answered every question with an extended technical answer. Once the engineer learned to respond concisely to questions, he quickly received an offer making 15 percent more money.

Bad assumptions can so intimidate you that you can be defeated before the fray begins. The only cure is to prepare as best you can and have the confidence that you can handle anything that arises. Don't compare yourself with other candidates because you don't know what the interviewer is looking for. Be yourself.

H. Anthony Medley, *Sweaty Palms:
The Neglected Art of Being Interviewed*

George A. Dow of Career Dynamics Inc. in Bloomington, Minnesota, describes a vice president whose job at a small medical technology firm was eliminated. The executive was 54 years old, with both engineering and M.B.A. degrees. In videotaped mock interviews, it was clear that while his verbal description of the reason for his departure was appropriate, the man was exhibiting angry body language. Watching himself on the monitor finally convinced him of the need to let go of his anger and move on with his life. He landed a new job six months later.

Acting lessons can enhance your self-confidence, enthusiasm and help you imbue a sense of drama into the interview process.

Make a list of the questions you most dread, and rehearse them on videotape until you and several objective observers are confident that you're conveying the proper image and message.

Eric Harvey, president of Dallas-based Performance Systems Corp., suggests that during the interview process, you match your own personal beliefs against the organization's stated beliefs, then observe to see if the organization's stated beliefs are being practiced. For example, if the company states that it's interested in employee development, does it conduct 360-degree feedback? If it's concerned with family balance, does it provide daycare services? If it professes an interest in wellness, is there a gym? The cultural match, Harvey says, may be more important in the employer's decision than the skills match.

Jonathan Spatt, president of Hospitality Executive Search in Boston, found the ideal candidate for a corporate executive chef position with a major hotel company at an annual salary of $260,000. After five interviews, the candidate met with the chief executive officer for dinner. When the CEO salted his soup without tasting it, the candidate returned to California, politely telling the recruiter he couldn't work for a company where the CEO didn't value the quality of the chef's cooking. That's honoring your values!

The Event Strategy is an essential tool for any kind of success . . . the key is that you can jump to the next plateau in your career when at least three career events occur in a concentrated period of time.

Ken Kragen, *Life Is a Contact Sport*

Here's a similar story, with a less happy ending. A candidate for a senior executive position at a large health care organization asked the CEO during the interview process, "How well will I be supported in my decisions during the first year?" Despite a lukewarm response, the candidate took the job. It was a troubled relationship from the start, exacerbated by a growing power struggle with a laterally reporting executive.

The new executive's first major action was recruiting an operating manager. After extensive interviews and approval of the selection by the CEO, an offer was extended. At this late date, however, the other manager intervened with objections, and the CEO reversed himself. The new executive realized that this was a crucial test of power, but was unwilling to bring a new manager into a potentially hostile environment. The offer was withdrawn. Within six months, the new executive himself was fired.

Interviews aren't won or lost on the basis of first impressions, despite what you might read in some books on interviewing. Employers today need results, not images. Never let your suspicion that an interview started awkwardly interfere with your mission of exploring common interests and explaining to the employer why you're the best person to meet his or her needs.

Richard H. Beatty, in his book *The Five Minute Interview,* describes a strategy that may help you frame and direct the interview process. Early in the interview, preferably before you're asked substantive questions, Beatty suggests that you try to frame the discussion with questions like these:

▶ What are the key strategic objectives of the organization?

▶ What are the key shifts or changes in direction that the organization is attempting to bring about?

▶ How will these changes affect the expectations of the department in which I will be working?

▶ How will the responsibilities of this position likely change over the next year?

It's important that you allow the interviewer to ask his or her questions, and that you ask your questions in a tactful way.

On the other hand, Douglas B. Richardson, a Philadelphia-based career consultant and author of the *National Business Employment Weekly's Premier Guide to Networking,* cautions against trying too hard to take control of the interview—an approach he says almost always fails. A successful interview, he says, is more than just a sales pitch for getting a job offer. It should be a collaborative process to provide both the employer and the candidate with the information they need to make an informed, intelligent and accurate decision about the possibility of working together.

Unfortunately, there will be times when the interviewer is unprepared or inept. Patricia B. Carr, a human resources specialist in Pittsburgh, suggests treating a job interview as an important business trip, using these four steps:

1. Use the resume as a map to guide interviewers toward your most important qualifications.

2. Point out attractions, especially during an unstructured interview. Guide the interviewer toward your key strengths and attributes.

3. Watch out for detours, which include inappropriate or illegal questions, or allowing the interviewer to ramble off the topic.

4. If you're lost, ask for directions. If you're not sure where the interview is going, ask a question to give it new focus.

A friend of mine, a Boston recruiter, likes to ask this question, 'Well, what did you DO today?' He tells me he eliminates more prospects on the basis of this answer to this one than any other question in his arsenal.

Harvey Mackay, *Sharkproof*

In the book *Executive Job Search Strategies,* Robert C. Bruce describes a dozen ways that interviewers are likely to evaluate an interviewee:

1. Experience in operating successfully with a team.

2. Follow-through and commitment.

3. Emotional stability and even temperament.

4. Self-confidence.

5. Conscientiousness.

6. Honesty and sincerity.

7. Maturity.

8. Adaptability and ability to manage multiple commitments.

9. Aggressiveness.

10. Self-discipline and sense of urgency.

11. Work ethic.

12. Tough-mindedness and high, demanding standards.

During the interview, actively search for objections you may have to overcome. Get them out on the table. Only when potential objections are expressed and understood can you effectively counter them. If they aren't obvious, consider asking a question like: "Given your review of my credentials and our interview, what would be your greatest reservation about offering me this job?"

Here's a key interview question: "What *projects* will I be able to work on?" In the future, people will build their careers around projects, not successive rungs on a ladder of success. Make sure that you'll have the opportunity to work on appropriate projects.

Arlene Hirsch, a career counselor and psychotherapist in Chicago, and author of the *National Business Employment*

Weekly's Premier Guide to Interviewing, emphasizes the importance of relationship interviewing. She says that "this approach equalizes the relationship so that it feels more like two adult human beings having a conversation." In the process, it also accomplishes what should be one of your primary objectives of interviewing: to determine whether this is a good job for you.

During the interview, one technique for creating rapport is to subtly mirror the person with whom you're interviewing. In his book *Unlimited Power,* Anthony Robbins states that 55 percent of effective communication is body language, including facial expressions, gestures and movement. "Studies of successful people," he says, "have shown over and over that they have a great talent for creating rapport. If you can see and hear and feel, you can create rapport with anyone just by doing what he [or she] does. You're looking for the things you can mirror as unobtrusively and naturally as possible."

The main focus of the five-minute interview concept is on the strategic goals and objectives of the organization. You must therefore have some understanding of where the organization is headed before you can effectively position yourself as someone who can help bring about positive change within the organization.

Richard H. Beatty, *The Five Minute Interview*

Judge the company by who's involved in the interview process. At Microsoft, senior executives participate in interviewing even newly graduated computer programmers. Interviewing is conducted by hiring managers, not human resources staff. This sends a powerful message to prospective employees that they'll be a part of the team and have access to senior management.

During the interview, pay attention as though your life depended on it. Keep asking yourself "how is this going?" Suspend your judgment, both concerning your performance and what you're hearing from the interviewer. You can make judgments later—now is the time to be objective.

Have a 30-second "commercial" for yourself. Following is one developed by Ronda J. Ormont in an article she wrote for the *National Business Employment Weekly:*

> Let me introduce myself. My name is Ronda Ormont. I am an experienced career development specialist with expertise in all aspects of vocational counseling, including knowledge of the business world, resume writing and interviewing techniques. I have a doctorate in psychology, conduct job-search programs and write articles for professional publications.

That is a powerful way to start an interview.

Appreciate the power of your voice, and understand that you can work to develop a more effective and pleasing voice. One way is to order the five-cassette program *Vocal Awareness* by voice specialist Arthur Joseph from the Sounds True Company (800-333-9185).

We all get better with practice. Don't let your first interview be with the company you most want to work for. Get your flubs and faux pas out of the way in interviews that don't mean as much to you.

The Five-Point Agenda is a predetermined analysis in which you select your five most marketable points and repeatedly

weave these points throughout the interview process. It's this repetition and reiteration of exactly how you'll meet their needs that allows the employer to remember something about you.

Robin Ryan, *60 Seconds and You're Hired*

If you simply can't seem to get your emotions under control, try hypnosis. One senior executive who had recently been fired had an interview scheduled with a key recruiter. He found it exceedingly difficult to conceal his anger at the way the firing was handled and his worries about the future. The day before the interview, he worked with an experienced hynotherapist, who helped him visualize himself conducting the interview with poise and professionalism. That's exactly how it went.

Take notes during each interview, and save them for future reference. One executive was asked by a recruiter to list her most important values. Though she hadn't prepared for the question, she extemporized well. Fortunately, after the interview, she wrote down the conversation in her journal. Several years later, when the same recruiter asked her the same question, she was prepared to respond in a way that was consistent with the first response.

Sheila Reilly was an employee with IBM Corp. when she was interviewed by telephone for a job with Silicon Graphics in Mountain View, California. By having extensively researched the company and preparing her own questions, she was able to allow the interviewer do much of the talking—for example, answering questions about the kind of people who had been hired in the past. She got the job.

If the interview has gone well and you're interested in the job, enthusiastically say that you want it ("It's been a pleasure meeting you and your associates. The job seems perfect, and I know we would enjoy working together."). Then ask about the process: How many other people are being interviewed? Where do I stand? What are the next steps? What's the timetable likely to be?

Be prepared for the behavioral or competency-based interview, which are increasingly being used by employers. Behavior-based interviews are much more difficult to bluff your way through because the questions require a specific example for a response. A typical question might be, "Tell me about a time that you disagreed with your boss, and how you handled it."

There's no such thing as an ad that gives too hard a sell. Don't soft-sell your product—you probably can't afford it.

Seth Godin, *Business Rules of Thumb*

Paul Green, president of Behavioral Technology, in Memphis, Tennessee, provides his clients with nearly 200 competency-based interview questions. One way to prepare for behavior-based interviews is to make a list of specific experiences that demonstrate the following:

▶ Teamwork.

▶ Leadership.

▶ Values and integrity.

▶ Work ethic.

▶ Results orientation.

▶ Flexibility and adaptability.

▶ Resilience.

▶ Technical acumen (finance, marketing, personnel and others).

▶ Personal attributes (equanimity, sense of humor, tolerance, tough-mindedness and others).

A ccording to Chicago career counselor Arlene Hirsch, a thank-you letter should be more than a polite note. It should be a powerful selling tool. She suggests the following four-part structure to get the most effective message across:

1. Tell the interviewer how much you enjoyed the meeting.

2. Express your enthusiasm for the company and the job.

3. Reiterate a specific selling point.

4. Establish your next point of contact.

O pinions differ as to whether the best thank-you notes are handwritten or typed. Unless you sense a highly informal culture, the best bet is probably to type them on monarch-sized stationery. Thank-you letters should be in the mail the day following the interview. Send one to every person you met, including the person who escorted you from one interview to another.

S everal days after the interview, consider making a call to see if, in thinking things over, the hiring authority has any additional questions that you might clarify.

I f you're asked to take a personality test, take it. You could learn some valuable information about yourself, and possibly prevent serious problems by avoiding taking a job at a company where you wouldn't fit in. If an employer is asking you to take the test, he or she thinks it's important.

High achievers tend to act differently than their underachieving colleagues. You might say that the high achievers exude a different sense of interpersonal drama or theater in the ways that they interact with other people. In other words, "showmanship."

Michael W. Mercer, *How Winners Do It*

Here's a great idea from Adele Scheele, Ph.D., a career strategist in New York. If you don't get a job after having made it to the final interview stage, send another gracious thank-you note stating how impressed you were with the company, and then call to suggest that the interviewer pass your name along to others in the company who might be looking for an excellent employee.

There are a number of books with listings of potential interview questions. *Knock 'Em Dead* by Martin Yate includes more than 200 tough interview questions and suggested responses. The *National Business Employment Weekly's Premier Guide to Interviewing* by Arlene S. Hirsch is an excellent overview of the process. *Sweaty Palms: The Neglected Art of Being Interviewed* by H. Anthony Medley includes great strategies for building self-confidence and interviewing effectively.

There are firms that will check your references for you (some run advertisements in the *National Business Employment Weekly*). If you think that one of your references is hurting your job-search efforts, you can consider contacting one of these firms to check for you. Remember, however, that you should always notify your references and prepare them for any call. You're either going to have to let that slip or twist the truth beyond what may be comfortable for you to do.

Career counselor Art Rimback suggests including powerful and influential people on your reference list, but save them for the job opportunities that really count.

Keep your perspective after a disappointing rejection. Warren Buffet was discouraged after being rejected by the Harvard Business School, but was accepted by Columbia. There he met Benjamin Graham, who helped mold his investment philosophy and early experiences. He now considers being rejected by Harvard as one of the luckiest experiences of his life.

A person who's trying to achieve the pleasure of success without ever experiencing the pain of rejection will never succeed long term. In fact, this person will sabotage himself before he ever truly succeeds on a major scale.

Anthony Robbins, *Awaken the Giant Within*

Studies of human communications show that only 7 percent of what is conveyed is by words; 38 percent of the communication effect is tone of voice, and fully 55 percent is body language. Be animated during interviews. Use body movements, hand gestures and facial expressions to convey your enthusiasm for the opportunity. An interview isn't an academic interchange; it's a performance.

If you have certain strong values (for example, regarding the environment, equal opportunity and so on), ask point-blank about these during the interview, especially if your research has indicated reasons that you should be concerned. The company will probably respect you for your forthrightness, and if it doesn't, having asked the questions may prevent you from becoming entangled in an impossible conflict of values should you get the job.

Try reversing the behavioral interview approach by asking the interviewer questions requiring a case study answer, such as: "Tell me about a time when this organization faced a conflict between its core philosophy regarding people and its responsibility to maximize return to shareholders."

If you've got a full day of interviews, there might be one person you feel comfortable asking to go with you for a walk while you talk. This will help keep you refreshed, and help differentiate you from the rest of the field ("he's the one who had the energy to take me for a walk").

Beginning as soon as you know about the interview, use mental visioning to create a memory of the future. First, use deep breathing and meditation to relax. Recall past instances of successful interviews in as vivid detail as possible. Visualize yourself answering questions with confidence and authority, smiling often and laughing easily, and knocking their socks off. Picture in your mind being invited back for another interview, with the inevitable outcome that you'll be offered the job.

Sometimes a stress interview is, in fact, an interviewer's tool to assess your behavior in high-pressure situations. And at other times, it's a preview of what the job will be like.

Gregory F. Farrell, *A Funny Thing Happened at the Interview*

Before every interview, review the skills of effective listening:

1. Listen attentively, and let the speaker know you're doing it by leaning forward slightly and maintaining good eye contact.

2. Don't do all the talking. Try to ask at least one question for every two that you answer.

3. Discipline your mind not to wander.

4. Don't interrupt.

5. Before you speak, pause for a breath and to put yourself in a thoughtful frame of mind.

6. Ask questions for clarification.

7. Periodically paraphrase what you hear the interviewer telling you.

The newspaper photograph of Ronald Reagan sitting at a speaker's dais with a hole in his shoe did no harm to his presidential candidacy; indeed, it probably helped. Old shoes won't help your job candidacy, however. What's on your feet should look like they just came out of the box.

If you happen to be interviewed at a time when some special occasion occurs—such as Secretary's Day or Valentine's Day—send a card to all the secretaries you've met during the interview process.

During the interview, listen for the company's "hot buttons." If you hear a term such as productivity, quality or ethics mentioned more than once, make a point of describing your attributes along that dimension in every interview.

Studies have shown that, other things being equal, people are more likely to buy something from a clean-shaven salesman. If you have a beard or mustache, at least consider the possibility of shaving it off until you're safely situated in the new job.

Prior to every important interview, prepare a "checklist." Include on this everything you need to bring. Go through it as religiously as an airline pilot (hopefully!) does. That way, you'll never find yourself in a strange hotel room with no dress shoes half an hour before an interview.

Fear of rejection can create a self-fulfilling prophecy. Take a warrior's attitude with you into the interview: "It's a great day to die!" Do your best, have fun, and what will be will be.

In the evening after each interview, replay the meeting(s), but put yourself in the perspective of the person on the other side of the desk(s). Without being critical or judgmental, how do you think they perceived your performance, and what can you learn to do better next time? This is great material to record in your journal.

Spend no more than a few minutes on chitchat and then get to the point—ask questions about the position, present your qualifications, and when the interviewer talks, listen.

Gregory F. Farrell, *A Funny Thing Happened at the Interview*

"Crenshaw, give that contract back to Higgins . . . he touched it first so his germs are on it!"

11
On the Job

Don't think of your new job as a job, but as a series of projects. As long as you have projects to work on that bring more value to your employer than the cost of retaining you, you're probably secure. Go out of your way to earn invitations onto project teams, to think up new projects that create value and to successfully complete the projects you tackle. Attack your work with relentless enthusiasm, but also refrain from taking the job for granted, since you never know when your next project will be to find a new job.

The people who actually do most of the knowledge and service work in organizations—engineers, teachers, salespeople, nurses, middle managers in general—carry a steadily growing load of busywork, additional activities that contribute little or no value and that have little or nothing to do with what these people are qualified and paid for . . . this is not job enrichment; it's job impoverishment.

Peter F. Drucker, *Manager for the Future*

Goodrich & Sherman, a New York human resources consulting firm, conducted a survey of 200 major companies and found that 90 percent of executives polled cited negative attitudes as one of the main reasons people get fired. On the new job, be open, cheerful, optimistic and receptive.

Don't be invisible! It may not come naturally to you to blow your own horn, but there are tactful ways it can be done. Try these:

1. Recognize the teams on which you're a member, which implicitly means you recognize yourself.

2. Keep a file of your accomplishments.

3. Schedule regular progress review meetings with your boss.

4. Be prepared for performance reviews.

5. Know the market value of your time.

6. Keep your boss informed of significant accomplishments.

7. Take on more work than is expected.

8. Assume projects that no one else wants.

9. Publicize your goals.

10. Do good deeds and random acts of kindness.

Cartoonist Scott Adams, creator of the Dilbert syndicated cartoon strip, was asked by *The Wall Street Journal* career columnist Hal Lancaster about the skills that get people promoted. He replied:

> Not counting sucking up? The best way to success is to look, act and dress like the person promoting you. I don't see that changing any time soon. The next best thing is to figure out what's important from what's not important. That's one of those things not everybody can do, but everybody can recognize it when you do it.

*By pressuring employees to produce in a narrowly measured way,
threatening them with loss of their jobs if they do not, and offering large rewards if they do, organization occasionally set individuals against each other and against their customers, with
catastrophic results.*

Jeffrey Pfeffer, *Competitive Advantage through People*

You dressed for the job you wanted, and you got it. Now, dress
for the future job to which you aspire. What are the incum-
bents of those jobs, your mentors and role models wearing? If you
want to get to where they are, dressing like they do would be a good
start.

Elizabeth Oleson, director of client services in the Newport
Beach, California, office of EnterChange, a national career
consulting firm, suggests the following seven steps to overcome
hidden obstacles on the new job:

1. Identify potential problems before acting.

2. Validate why you were hired, including seeking more detail
   than you were able to get in the interview.

3. Get to know your staff; what are their concerns, goals, ideas,
   and how can you facilitate their progress?

4. Understand and be sensitive to office culture.

5. Build alliances and your internal network.

6. Develop suitable goals, and don't try to perform miracles.

7. Implement your programs, keeping your boss and staff informed.

Take some time and review the basics. The longer you've been
in a career, the more likely it is that you're taking the basics
for granted, running the risk of making dumb mistakes.

Try to spend as much time as possible in direct communications, preferably face to face, with associates, customers and other key people. Save administrative work for slow time, bunch it together and learn to be more efficient. Do it at times when you can't be face to face with others.

Once you get the basics of your job under control, begin to volunteer for additional work. Patch together a bigger job from pieces of work that no one else wants to do.

Continue to learn new computer skills. If you don't make the time, you run the risk of getting farther and farther behind the technological curve, and you may despair of ever catching up.

Walter Polsky, CEO of Cambridge Resources Group in Chicago, suggests the following steps to get ahead on the job: accept in-house volunteer assignments; save your company money; work longer hours; be visible; be congenial.

Radiant thinking demonstrates that . . . the more you educate people, the more unique their vast, and growing, networks of [mental] associations become.

Tony Buzan, *The Mind Map Book*

Create a department or group newsletter for internal distribution, and send copies to your out-of-company networking contacts.

Start training your replacement immediately, so that not having someone to smoothly fill your shoes won't hold you back from your own promotion.

After you've started a new job, notify everyone who helped you. Wait a few weeks, however, to make sure you don't trip over any last-minute snags.

Give recognition and positive feedback to your bosses and lateral colleagues, not just downward.

Get 360-degree feedback often. Ask your boss, peers and subordinates how you're doing and what you could be doing better. But don't ask if you're not serious about considering the changes they might suggest.

Read annual reports, 10Ks, press releases and other materials from your company and all its competitors.

Spend the day with members of the younger generation, and ask yourself these questions: What could I sell them? How could I employ them?

Gordon F. Shea, president of Prime Systems Co. in Beltsville, Maryland, and author of *Mentoring: Helping Employees Reach*

Their Full Potential, provides the following guidelines for choosing a mentor. Select people:

▶ Who aren't interested in using you for empire building.

▶ Who have their own successful careers.

▶ Who are good teachers and enjoy sharing their secrets of success.

▶ Who thoroughly understand corporate policy, goals, politics and culture.

Never rely on a mentor for your career progress. Ideally, mentors should be someone outside of your direct chain of command.

During your early weeks on a new job, don't feel you have to be an immediate success. You don't, and in most cases you can't.

Carol Kleiman, *The Career Coach*

Following are times when you should consider leaving the organization:

▶ You've been demoted.

▶ Your salary's been decreased.

▶ The boss ignores you.

▶ You lose responsibilities.

▶ You don't know what's going on, or are surprised by major announcements.

▶ The division or your company is failing financially.

Remember the words of the *I Ching:* "When one purges oneself of vanity and arrogance and awakens to the value of subordination, one can approach a teacher with an unassuming attitude and obtain subsequent enlightenment." Or, as the Zen masters put it, when the student is ready, the teacher appears.

Sometimes it's necessary to cut your losses quickly. When Joe Brown, 31, lost his job as vice president of operations for an apparel company, he began analyzing whether to start his own business. When an opportunity arose with another company, however, he accepted it. After only several weeks on the job, it was clear that it wouldn't work out. He quit the company, and using his house as collateral for a loan, he started his own children's retail store in Connecticut. The company grew by adding outlets, and five years later he sold it to a large chain, staying on to manage the division's continued growth.

Deborah Zeigler of Greenberg Zeigler Associates in Teaneck, New Jersey, describes a man who had been a vice president in his company for 10 years. He was highly regarded for his technical skills, but his management style was rigid, and he was so uncomfortable with his boss' directness that he developed strong physical reactions such as facial ticks, grimaces and stuttering. The VP was given an ultimatum: seek counseling to modify inappropriate behaviors or lose the job.

Through the process of personality testing, role-playing and counseling, he learned new ways to deal with his emotions, with conflict and with alliance building. More important, he learned to relax and detach himself emotionally, which helped him eliminate his inappropriate behaviors. He kept the job for another five years before deciding to start his own business, with his former employer being one of several clients.

Judy Hamilton of Schonberg Associates in Hamilton, Indiana, describes a case that starkly illustrates the importance of understanding corporate politics. A nationally known, family-owned health insurance company had decided to release its archivist. His skills were excellent, but his personality didn't mesh with a key family member. The archivist didn't like playing games, and was unwilling to treat the family member with the deference she expected. Though he was shocked and angered at being fired, he subsequently realized that he should have seen it coming; in a family-owned firm, not being liked by a key family member is probably a job killer.

Mahatma Gandhi once wrote that there were seven sins in the world: wealth without work; pleasure without conscience; knowledge without character; commerce without morality; science without humanity; worship without sacrifice; politics without principle. Performance considered in light of those seven sins would be well-reviewed performance indeed.

Max DePree, *Leadership Is an Art*

Sam Bennett was terminated by a large international food producer after a 27-year career with the company. He began as a clerk and worked his way up to regional manager. When the position was eliminated, Bennett quickly realized that because his entire career had been spent with one company, he would have to build his network from scratch. Fortunately, he was able to find a temporary position that allowed him to make many contacts, which ultimately resulted in a new permanent position.

Scott R. McFaddin, an outplacement associate with Murray Axmith and Associates LTD in Toronto, describes a case that highlights the dangers of being disconnected with your boss. A 45-year-old executive was fired as editor of a Canadian publishing company after 15 years with the organization. A new manager was brought in with a style perceived as autocratic. Because of his differences with the new boss, the editor began to avoid him, allowing channels of communication to fade. This led the manager to perceive him as being unmotivated, resulting in his termination.

Start a book review and discussion club within the company.

Make lateral moves within the company if a firing is on the horizon.

Think twice about opportunities to be relocated, especially if a promotion and a pay raise aren't included. Relocations can result in a reduced standard of living and significant family disruption. And if the job disappears a year or two later, you're stuck in a city where you have few contacts.

Don't wind down your job search until you've been established in the new job for at least a week, and don't send out a general notification for at least two weeks.

It was clear from [our] investigation that an expectation gap *exists between managers and new employees. Employees expected to receive more direction from their managers than they, in fact, received; managers expected to give less direction. The result of the expectation gap is that many new employees find themselves floundering in their new work environments, often making key, nontechnical errors.*

Lynda Clemens and Andrea Dolph, *How to Hit the Ground Running in Your New Job*

Before you were hired, you had to convince the people above you in the organization that you were the right person for the job. After being hired, your task is to convince the rest of the organization that those people made the right decision. The best way is to listen, appreciate who people are and what they've accomplished, give them pride in their work and gain their confidence. Work long hours at first to be visible and to get to know everyone. Target a few early successes to start building your momentum.

New York career counselor Shirley Sloan Fader says that a new boss will expect you to do the following 20 things:

1. Get the work done on time without making excuses.

2. Get the job done—even if it's not perfect.

3. Take initiative and do more than expected.

4. Anticipate and prepare for troubles and problems.

5. Handle problems, not pass them upstairs.

6. Be on time.

7. Take your work seriously.

8. Don't complain.

9. Choose your battles with care.

10. Continue to be a team player, even when you lose.

11. Work with decision makers to get action.

12. Understand what the boss really wants.

13. Learn to understand the big picture and your role in it.

14. Get along with people.

15. Protect confidentiality.

16. Develop a good sense of timing.

17. Be honest and protect your credibility.

18. Stay on top of industry trends and read the trade press.

19. Get to know your peers.

20. Don't assume—check things out personally.

Make your boss look like a hero and give your staff credit for doing it.

NEGOTIATION

Negotiation does not begin *until you have a written job offer in hand . . . . If an offer is not made, you don't negotiate and you definitely keep your job search active.*

Charles H. Logue, *Outplace Yourself: Secrets of an Executive Outplacement Counselor*

When negotiating the terms for a new position, remind yourself that if everything works out, you'll be working with these people. Be nice!

When negotiating for a job in today's environment, think 1 to 2 years, not 5 to 10. Think cash compensation, not perks and benefits. Think "pay for measurable performance," not "vague promises of a future review."

If the base offer is insufficient, ask for something you can earn— pay for performance, incentive compensation, cash bonuses or stock options.

Avoid asking for perks that can be seen as extravagant, especially when companies want to be seen as cost conscious. Demanding a country club membership when people are losing their jobs might be bad form.

What you see during negotiations might be your first true indicator of what it's like to work for that employer. If you don't like what you see, walk away.

One of the best common sense books on negotiation is *Roger Dawson's Secrets of Power Negotiating.* One of the key principles that Dawson describes is trying to get the other side to make an offer before you do. The less you know about what might be offered, the more important it is to not go first.

Brad M. Buchlin, a career development and resume specialist with Career Pro Professional Literary Service in Los Angeles, suggests this exercise to convince employers of your market value: first, make a written list of your skills and knowledge. If you have skills or knowledge in more than one area, make separate lists to see which items overlap. Next, research the market by calling target companies and talk with people doing jobs like the one for which you're interviewing. Compare their backgrounds with yours and get a ballpark salary range. Get as much information as possible, especially since salary ranges are likely to be broad. A spin-off benefit of this approach is that you'll add people to your network.

Take this advice from Paul Hawkinson, publisher of the *Fordyce Letter,* a St. Louis-based monthly newsletter for the executive search and placement fields: "The litany of horror stories I've come across in my years as an executive recruiter, consultant and publisher provides a litmus test that clearly indicates counteroffers should never be accepted . . . EVER!"

The most important thing you should negotiate is the content and responsibility of your job, not the money.

In a *National Business Employment Weekly* article, senior editor Perri Capell tells the story of Kathleen Strickland, who was laid off from a $125,000 job as a senior vice president with a retailer. She was offered a position with another firm at $60,000, which she declined. She subsequently declined follow-up offers of $80,000, and $100,000, before finally accepting an offer at $130,000. Strickland was successful, says Capell, because "she knew it was a negotiation from the start, was incredibly specific, set her priorities and was willing to walk away if she didn't get them."

Negotiate cash first, benefits second and perquisites last.

The longer you can put off talking about money during the interview/negotiation process, the better off you're likely to be.

Don't accept a job offer without sleeping on it.

Paul Hellman, *Savvy*

"I'm afraid we'll have to let you go, Stan . . . you're just not making enough noise."

12

Coping with Setbacks

Michael Jordan was cut from his high school basketball team; Babe Ruth struck out nearly twice for every home run he hit; Colonel Sanders was rejected more than 1,000 times before, at age 67, he sold his first Kentucky Fried Chicken franchise. You may stumble and fall, but you won't fail as long as you refuse to quit. How you cope with setbacks will be one of the most important determinants of your future career success.

A Nobel prize-winner once proved that a cell changes or grows only after going through a period of vulnerability. It was called the "rock bottom" theory. It's only after you hit rock bottom that you achieve the prudence, confidence and adaptability needed to grow and succeed.

Stephen Phillips, *Success* magazine "Great Comebacks" honoree

When Robert Schuller's family farm was utterly destroyed by a tornado, his father—who was 65 years old and walked with a cane—told his 19-year-old son to get a good night's rest, because in the morning they would start over. "Start over?" Schuller asked. "With what? There's nothing left." After a long moment of silence, his father replied, "Never look at what you've lost. Always look at what you have left." They bought a vacant house for $50, dismantled it board by board, and reassembled it on their property. If you lose a job, look at what you've got left, not at what you've lost. Then add faith, energy and determination to build your new future.

Go to your library and read the "Great Comebacks" issue of *Success* magazine for the past 10 years.

One of the most profound song series I've ever heard on dealing with setbacks is *Job, the Winter Traveler* by Doug Peters. This is one of a series of tapes that Rev. Peters has recorded around Biblical themes. In particular, the song "You're (Tough As) Nails" has been a great courage builder. Doug's tapes can be obtained through Paradox 21 Press at 800-644-3889.

Susanne Kobasa and her colleagues at the University of Chicago studied executives at AT&T Co. during several corporate reorganizations and downsizings. While some executives had their health adversely affected by the stress, others held up well. The latter group shared the following three qualities:

1. They had a strong commitment to both work and family.

2. Although they couldn't control the details of work, they felt they still had control of the overall quality of their lives, and that whatever happened, they had options for action.

3. They viewed change as a challenge, not a threat.

It was, in summary, their optimistic attitude that carried them through stressful times.

The ability to forgive and the ability to love are the weapons God has given us to live fully, bravely and meaningfully in this less-than-perfect world.

Harold Kushner, *When Bad Things Happen to Good People*

If you lose a job, be cautious before investing time and money into becoming more highly specialized in any field. According to a recent article in *Forbes* magazine, sophisticated computer software will increasingly be able to replace the skills of many professionals who use algorithmic thinking in their jobs. This includes lawyers, doctors, computer programmers and other professions once considered relatively recession-proof. For example, the Will-Maker computer program of Nolo Press has written more wills than any lawyer alive.

Check to see if your local church or synagogue sponsors a job-support group. Becoming part of a group like this can help you with emotional support, additional networking contacts and, most important, help keep you focused on what's really important. According to Michael Parsells, an executive recruiter in Menlo Park, California, staying focused on your spiritual mission in life is certain to lead you toward the right job. For a current list of job clubs nationwide, see the Calendar of Events section in the *National Business Employment Weekly.*

Buy and read the books *Take Courage; Be Stouthearted: Psalms of Support and Encouragement* by William J. Byron and *Psalms for Times of Trouble* by John Carmody.

Lori is an alcoholic. At 33 years old, she'd always worked as a waitress and used drinking to escape from insecurities, bad marriages and sad memories. Finally, she decided to confront her problems with courage, and stop drinking. This has given her the faith and equanimity to believe in herself and her future. "When I was drinking," she says, "the end of the world was always right around the corner. Now I know I can make a rational choice. There's always something you can do."

When two things happen after having lost a job, you'll know that you're well along the path toward recovery and changing your focus from past anger to future hope. First, you'll begin to admit to yourself the ways in which your own behaviors, attitudes and failures contributed to your loss of the job—even if it's just to acknowledge that had you been better prepared, you at least would have seen it coming. Second, you'll have let go of the need to blame those who fired you, and forgive them for doing what they believed they had to do.

Rich Emerson left an executive position with a major university alumni department in 1994. At a loss concerning what to do next, he accepted a job with the local office of a major regional stock brokerage firm. Although the work itself wasn't particularly fulfilling, he learned a great deal about business and finance. This new knowledge, coupled with his experience managing at several nonprofit organizations, led within a year to a job offer as executive director of a small-town Chamber of Commerce.

The three negative outcomes of being fired that almost no one avoids are depression, isolation and self-blame.

Barry Glassner, *Career Crash*

If being fired three times has taught him anything, Harold Bischoff has learned that people are more in control of their lives than they give themselves credit for. At various times, he worked in manual construction, sold homes and prepared taxes. In the late '80s, recognizing that managed care would dominate the health care landscape, he began to direct his career into that area. In 1990, he accepted a job as executive director of Healthwise of Kentucky. In 1996, his company merged with a larger organization, and now has plans to spin off his division into a separate public corporation.

Keep your family informed. Mike Broscio of Career Decisions, a Chicago-based outplacement firm specializing in health care, tells of a man who was fired with a two-year severance package. Every day for two years, he put on a suit and traveled to the outplacement office. Unfortunately, during this entire time, he never informed his wife that he'd lost his job. When the severance ran out and he was still unemployed, there was major trauma on the homefront!

Christine McMorrow of Mahwah, New Jersey, was downsized and received two months of outplacement counseling services. At the end of the two months, she wanted to extend her time there, but couldn't afford the cost. She offered to barter her writing skills by running writing workshops and one-on-one sessions. She would teach candidates how to write cover letters in return for continued outplacement counseling and use of the facility. This was, she says, a win-win solution that not only provided her with continued outplacement services, but also helped her develop solid presentation skills, networking contacts and increased self-confidence.

Ken Gomez was a fire inspector at the James Fitzpatrick Nuclear Power Plant in New York when he was laid off. Fortunately, he was ready. He'd been moonlighting for Primerica Financial Services (PFS) for the previous 18 months. He loved that job, as well as the people he worked with, but hadn't felt ready to quit his "real job" to do it full time. Now he says that getting laid off was a blessing, because it forced him to concentrate on building his business at PFS, which has been successful beyond his expectations.

A part of your journey will be acknowledging your own short-comings and faults, and seeking forgiveness. This is a healthy thing, but it's not healthy to dwell upon your guilt. Instead, resolve to make the changes necessary to live right and work right.

Dealing with trauma seems to require at least two crucial elements: reliving the experience and transformation of the trauma.

Joan Borysenko, *Fire in the Soul*

P aul Abbott spent 10 years as a commodity trader on the Chicago Board of Options. He liked the work, but hated the daily commute and the stressful lifestyle. He and his wife Linda both longed for a change, so in 1989, they sold their home and bought a small lakeside resort in Wisconsin, looking forward to the simple life. Instead, what they got was a nightmare.

Business went bad, and they finally had to bail out. After two years, Paul got a job trading commodities for clients via phone and fax from his new home. He's now happier than ever, and is glad that he made the fateful mistake to buy the resort. "I don't think I would have ended up here if we first hadn't ended up there," he told *The Wall Street Journal.* "I'm glad we had the guts to do it."

H al Lancaster, career reporter for *The Wall Street Journal,* offers the following advice for anyone whose organization is involved in a merger:

1. Set aside any preconceptions about what the merger will mean, and take it as it comes.

2. Don't do anything rash.

3. Do some research about the new partner and its motivations.

4. Pay attention to organizational politics.

5. Simplify other areas of your life to cut back on stress.

6. Don't resist change because, chances are, you can't stop it.

7. Don't expect a smooth transition and quick answers.

8. Don't bury yourself in a foxhole—use the early days to make a good first impression on the new partners.

9. Be ready to leave if things aren't working out.

N ever stop reading industry and trade publications. If you can't afford the subscription costs, go to the library.

E very Sunday evening, make one "New Week's Resolution" for the coming week.

D on't believe gloomy forecasts of an America with no jobs; articles claiming that virtually everyone who loses a job these days slips down the socioeconomic scale; or that 9 out of 10 new business ventures fail. If you had the time (and you don't) to go back through the library archives, you'd find a steady stream of such articles have been written since the Great Depression. Despite them all, people have still been able to find better jobs, make better livings and start successful businesses, and you can too.

I f you're involved in working with support groups, don't become a workshop junkie who confuses this activity with real progress toward landing a job.

If we cannot forgive, we end up crucifying ourselves on the very cross we construct for our scapegoats. Our hate will be the hatred in ourselves that we've repressed, and that hatred of others masking our own self-hatred will continue to crucify us in their name.

Michael H. Crosby, *The Seven Last Words*

D r. N. Michael Markowich, a Huntington Valley, Pennsylvania,
human resources consultant, suggests a "preemptive strike" if
you believe your company would like to get rid of you. By approaching the employer, you might be in a better position to negotiate an adequate severance package. Ask yourself these questions:

▶ What's important to the employer?

▶ What potential damage could I do that they can head off with a
severance package?

▶ Am I in a highly visible position?

▶ What's my value to other organizations?

Be sure that you're right about being unwanted before broaching
the subject, or you could quickly create an unfortunate self-
fulfilling prophecy.

V irginia K. Gordon, a Chicago psychiatric social worker and
family therapist, suggests entering a three-part "Keep Kids
Safe" contract that provides for a tight parental alliance to protect
kids during a period of unemployment; assures that everyone will
pay attention to the family environment and offer and accept suggestions for improvements; and follow up with open discussion and
family meetings.

D ouglas B. Richardson, founder of Richardson & Co., a career
consulting firm in Bala Cynwyd, Pennsylvania, encourages
clients not to advertise to prospective employers that they're in
outplacement counseling. He suggests the following:

1. Speak for yourself, and don't let the outplacement counseling
firm write your cover letters or resume. Don't slavishly copy
their model cover letters.

2. Don't use the paper they offer; he says that 25-pound water-mark bond has come to be known as "outplacement ivory" by recruiters and human resources professionals.

3. Make changes to the resume format they recommend. If they suggest putting a mission statement at the top, don't do it, or at least call it something different.

4. Ask for a private phone line that is answered with your name, not "Executive Offices," and offer to pay the cost.

5. Don't use the scripts that they provide to you for networking, or interviewing; use your own words.

6. Don't overdue the dramatic body gestures they might recommend, betraying the fact that you've been coached.

Being fired could be viewed as an opportunity to take stock and to set out on the career path that will make you happiest and most productive during the latter portion of your working life.

Robert Half, *How to Get a Better Job in This Crazy World*

Be glad for what you've lost. Laura Bibby thought she was happy with her clerical job at a major public utility, until the company announced layoffs. For two months, nobody knew who would go, only that some of them would.

"You could imagine the morale in the office," she says. "I suddenly got the feeling that it was every person for themselves, and the only reason people came in to work was for a paycheck." Bibby was one of those let go. She eventually found a job working for a community-based bank, and now realizes that losing the job was "the best thing that could have happened to me." The new company, she says, has heart and soul, something she believes was lacking at the utility, where a bottom-line mentality prevailed.

Look for a crisis to work yourself out of your crisis. Anne Busquet was General Manager of the American Express Co. Optima card unit when it was discovered that some of her employees had committed accounting fraud. She was relieved of her job, and offered a position managing the company's distressed merchandise services division. She thought seriously about quitting, but instead plunged into the crisis-ridden unit and engineered a turnaround. She is now an executive vice president at the company, and is frequently cited as someone who was able to overcome career crisis by having the courage to take on a difficult challenge.

Richard McKnight, head of a consulting and training firm in Narbeth, Pennsylvania, says there are three typical reactions to organizational turmoil. First, some people see themselves as victims and respond with the fight or flight reflex. They often respond with hostility, fear and depression, and may be incapacitated and unwilling or unable to try training, networking or other activities that would help them. Second, survivors develop a fighting spirit. While this is better than being a victim, McKnight says, survivors are prone to burnout, denial and psychosomatic diseases. Finally, McKnight says that navigators accept the reality of their current situation and let go of the past quickly so that they can move on to a new future. A job-loss victim may go through all three stages, but it's best to become a navigator as quickly as possible.

If you're a recent survivor of a corporate downsizing, expect more work immediately and a period of seeming disorganization.

Sheriden Stolarz spent her entire life's savings in 1990 to follow a life-long dream of becoming a paralegal. She moved to Denver for six weeks and became certified, but upon her return to Los Angeles, she couldn't even schedule an interview. Depressed at having to work at a low-level job she didn't enjoy, she began volunteering with the Crystal Cathedral Ministries. This soon led to a job offer working in the development office, where she was able to use some of her paralegal skills helping with wills and estates.

When a new chief operating officer came on board, he asked her to head up the human resources function, which she did for a year. She is now assistant to the COO, which involves her in the group's entire range of activities. "Any experience is good experience," she now says. "Just find a need and fill it, and pretty soon your feet will be walking along the right path."

Bill Zimmerman lost his job as a senior vice president and editor at *American Banker* magazine in New York. At about the same time, his brother died of AIDS and his mother passed away. He started writing down positive thoughts, prayers, affirmations and wishes, which helped him overcome depression and stay more focused. He eventually got a job at *Newsday* newspaper, and his journal was just published by Hazelden under the title of *The Little Book of Joy.*

Being fired or terminated is rarely the outrageous, meaningless event that it at first seems to be . . . you have the power to shape it by how you chose to view it.

Richard Nelson Bolles, *The 1995 What Color Is Your Parachute?*

No matter how bad things seem, try to keep your perspective. Keep in mind the words of a young homeless teenage mother of two, who routinely had to stay up all night keeping rats and roaches away from her children: "People think they got it tough. They don't know the meaning of the word."

Two Zen monks were walking and came upon a young woman standing at the edge of a stream. One of the monks offered to carry her across. Several miles down the road, the other monk looked at his companion and said, "You shouldn't have carried that girl. It's against the rules of our order." To which the second monk replied, "I put her down hours ago. Are you still carrying her?"

Are you still carrying the dead weight of an ex-employer? Try this: close your eyes and visualize yourself carrying the old boss across the stream. On the other side, gently lay down your burden, say thank you for the lesson and leave it behind as you move down the road toward the rest of your life.

If you lose a job, think twice before getting another job doing the same old thing. Do your homework. Is the occupation you've been in going away? Are you simply delaying the inevitable need to bite the bullet and retrain and redirect yourself by taking another job in a dying profession?

In his book *Reawakening the Spirit at Work,* Jack Hawley points out that fear and anger always go together. There will never be one without the other. They feed on each other until you can't tell them apart. They'll destroy your objectivity and eventually your freedom of decision and action. That's why it's so important to confront your fear with courage and to calm your anger with love.

When you're feeling especially fragile, pull your ship into a harbor and hide out for a day or so.

The tip-of-the-iceberg rule is that, whenever something happens in your business or personal life, you should assume a trend *until proven otherwise.*

Brian Tracy, *Advanced Selling Strategies*

What do Billy Joel, Harold Hughes, Robert Fulghum, Buckminster Fuller and Paul Peterson have in common? They each almost committed suicide, then came around and realized that they had important work remaining undone. No matter how bad things seem, as long as you keep walking, you'll come out of the forest; as long as you keep climbing, you'll come to the top.

In his book *Listening to Prozac,* Peter D. Kramer describes a certain category of people who are hypersensitive to rejection. If your job search is stuck in the mud because you simply can't stand the possibility of more rejection, you might consider seeking professional help. "Rejection-sensitivity is both a manifestation of difficulties and a pathogen, causing further difficulties of its own," says Kramer.

There will be times during a prolonged job search when, no matter how faithful you are, it will feel like God has abandoned you. And perhaps that may be the case. If you're waiting around for divine intervention to plant your feet down on the right vocational path, or to open the right doors and arrange for lucrative job offers, your personal growth will depend upon you taking responsibility for yourself. Like a parent who ignores a whining, petulant child, God may just be waiting for you to grow up and start asking the right questions instead of asking for bailouts and handouts.

David Tetrault owns his own automotive transport business in Massachusetts. He's a hard-driving manager who does not like inactivity. After he fell 14 feet off the top of his truck and landed on his head, his doctors told him he was lucky to survive, and that he'd have to spend several weeks at home, resting. He acknowledged how lucky he was, but was also frustrated at being kept away from work. Finally, he realized he just had to accept it, let go and trust his doctors.

Sometimes, after losing a job, letting go is the only thing to do. Fighting it slows the healing process. Tetrault's experience of falling off the truck is a useful metaphor for falling off the job—sometimes you can't get right back up and return to work without a period of recuperation.

David M. Noer, senior vice president of the Center for Creative Leadership in North Carolina, says people who survive a downsizing often end up worse off than those who lost their jobs. In fact, he's named the syndrome "layoff survivor sickness," which is written about in his book *Healing the Wounds*.

The sickness of these people is often characterized by clusters of emotions including fear, insecurity and uncertainty; frustration, resentment and anger; sadness, depression and guilt; and unfairness, betrayal and distrust, he says. Not only do these feelings fail to go away over time, they intensify. Survivors become shell-shocked, fatigued and depressed and experience a deepening loss of control. If you've been let go in a downsizing, consider that you might be one of the lucky ones.

Involuntary loss of employment precipitated for me the most unhappy period of my life. My struggle with shame and unhealthy self-pity, loss of self-esteem and an inability to cope with rejection, however, did evolve into a determined search for methods to help others either prevent such occurrences or recover from them.

Paul Stevens, *Stop Postponing the Rest of Your Life*

Shoya Zichy quit a position as vice president of American Express Bank to devote herself full-time to painting. After several years, she returned to the corporate world as a consultant, where she found many extremely talented women who were terribly unhappy in their work. She started a new business combining personality testing and counseling, and in her first nine months, counseled more than 200 clients.

In a *Fortune* magazine article, Betsy Morris described many executive women confronting midlife crisis. Many of these women left the corporate world to start their own small businesses. Morris concludes, "That is how some experts believe women will have the most influence in business in the future—by doing things their way. It's the legacy that many in this generation of businesswomen hope to leave for the next: that they have options, can make changes and conduct business on their own terms."

Chris Spencer was fired from a 17-year job as a middle manager with a major Canadian financial institution as part of a corporate reorganization. After interviews, she was rejected for a position she really wanted. But her analysis of the interview process convinced her that the organization liked her. Though she continued her job search on other fronts, she maintained contact with the preferred organization. Shortly, a new opportunity opened up with the company and she was hired. Never quit, because as Chris Spencer learned, "No" doesn't always mean "No" forever.

Sometimes you need to let go of cherished dreams and yank yourself into the present need for action. Mary Louise Hubal of Productivity Training Network in San Anselmo, California, worked with a mechanical engineer who'd been terminated after 25 years with his company. He loved the firm, and held out the possibility that he'd be rehired. As time passed, however, he fell into a downward spiral of inaction leading to dwindling savings, depression and further inaction. He finally began an Amway distributorship, while continuing to use his engineering background for small consulting projects.

When adversity threatens to paralyze us, we need to reassert control by finding a new direction in which to invest psychic energy, a direction that lies outside the reach of external forces. Whenever aspiration is frustrated, a person still must seek a meaningful goal around which to organize the self.

> Mihaly Csikszentmihalyi, *Flow: The Psychology of Optimal Experience*

Sally Kilbourne of Wright Associates in San Bernadino, California, warns against becoming complacent after early success in a job search. She was providing outplacement support for an information systems professional who had been out of work for 10 months. Soon after his employment ended, he landed several interviews after responding to classified ads. This had given him false assurance that networking was unnecessary. Only after admitting that he needed to overcome emotional barriers and get involved in networking did he find a new job.

Dan Deveraux saw the loss of his job as vice president of a medium-sized mining company during an acquisition as an opportunity to do something new. He garnered a consulting contract with another mining company, and his work was so well received that he was offered the presidency of a subsidiary. Deveraux recognized, however, that he didn't want an administrative position. Instead, he negotiated a newly created position of chief geoscientist, which was more consistent with his desires for hands-on work and international travel.

Katie Cooney of Market Share Inc. in Minneapolis, describes a case illustrating the value of psychological intervention during job-loss crisis. During an 18-year career, the client failed to show any real growth on the job, yet became excessively dependent on the position and assumed she would be taken care of by the company. Her termination provoked feelings of fear and anger; the career counselor and psychologist allowed the displaced employee to vent her feelings, but then quickly tried to move her focus toward the future. It became evident that the former employee had skills and talents that weren't being utilized effectively at the old company. Once these were identified, she was able to move ahead with enthusiasm and confidence.

A 35-year-old associate at a law firm was terminated from her position, which she'd held since graduation nine years earlier. After working with New York career counselor Leslie Prager, she cataloged her proudest accomplishments and completed a variety of vocational tests indicating strong interest in the creative arts. The woman wasn't excited about returning to the "sweatshop" environment of a law firm, and ended up accepting a position in the entertainment industry, which, although paying 20 percent less than her previous job, was much more rewarding.

Loss, by itself, is not tragic. What is *tragic is the failure to grasp the opportunity which loss presents.*

Robert K. Greenleaf, *Servant Leadership*

Sometimes you need to read a good book. Donna M. Bennett of the Esquire Group in Minneapolis describes a lawyer who was asked to leave her firm because of declining business. She was given only three months notice after 12 years with the firm, and struggled with panic because she was the sole support of her family. Bennett had her client start a journal to record her feelings, and read the book *Feel the Fear and Do It Anyway* by Susan Jeffers. By first attending to her client's panic and self-esteem problems, Bennett was able to help her build a solid emotional foundation for a successful job search.

Hang tough. Walter Thom was 32 when he was laid off from an investment services company where he'd worked for eight years. Shortly after losing his job, he was offered a position at half his former salary. Fortunately, he didn't accept the job, and within several months found an opportunity meeting his requirements for both compensation and professional and personal development.

On the other hand, never be too quick to turn down a job just because it pays less than you're used to making. William J. Morin, former chairman of Drake Beam Morin Inc., says that sometimes it makes sense to "take a job to get a job," meaning that it's always easier to find a new position when you're working than when you're not.

When Pierre Tremblay was forced out of his position with a Canadian pharmaceutical company after 21 years, he had to overcome a perceived need to prove that the company had made a bad decision, so he looked for a similar job with a competitor. His job search was stuck until he was able to accept that he didn't have to prove anything to his old company, and that he could pursue his own dreams and destiny.

I'm convinced that persons burdened with the stress of job loss can have their burdens lightened, if not lifted, by seeing themselves in the literary portrayals of persons and situations not unlike their own—descriptions and metaphors—crafted by fine writers and poets whose insights into the human condition are available to anyone willing to read. The return on the time invested in this kind of reading is personal progress in getting a grip on life.

William J. Byron, *Finding Work without Losing Heart*

If you lose a job, it won't be long before you hear someone say, "It's the best thing that could ever happen." You may not believe it, but consider the story of Mary Brown, who lost her $34,000 job as an administrative assistant with a brewery. She had always dreamed of being a sports broadcaster, and accepted a significant decrease in income for a research assistant's job at a broadcasting company. As she learned more about the business, she began conducting interviews with professional athletes. Within four years, she was a broadcasting success, earning $125,000 annually.

In his book, *Besting Job Burnout,* Paul Stevens, founder of the Centre for Work Life Counseling in Australia, quotes one of his career counseling clients as follows:

> All the separate achievements in a period of career reassessment combine to produce in me a profound, personal revolution; together they built self-esteem and a sense of direction for my life. I grew, or pushed myself, out of a life pattern of depression, lassitude and anxiety—my greatest achievement of my life to date.

If you've lost a job, make it a personal and binding commitment that someday you'll look back upon the experience as the best thing that ever could have happened to you.

In his book, *The Road to Successful Living,* Louis Binstock cites what he considers to be the 10 most common causes of failure. Avoid these, and you'll likely do well:

1. Blaming other people for your problems rather than accepting personal responsibility for your own life.

2. Blaming yourself by engaging in self-pity rather than constructive action for improvement.

3. Not having goals, having low goals or waiting for "a break."

4. Choosing the wrong goals.

5. Trying to take shortcuts along the road to success.

6. Taking a long and meandering road, rather than moving straight toward your goals.

7. Neglecting little things.

8. Quitting too soon.

9. Carrying around the dead weight of past anger and bitterness.

10. Resting on your laurels.

G ive yourself a week to be alone with a pile of good books, a supply of pens and pads and your journal.

Ironically, candidates are often interviewed at a time when their belief in themselves and their abilities has been shaken. To maintain a positive attitude, a candidate must possess and be able to draw upon internal reserves; that same inner confidence and determination goes a long way toward insuring a manager's success.

Ron Shaw, President, Pilot Pen Corp. of America

I f you have an annoying cut or blister, it may seem like it's the very center of your existence, even though it's really just a very small part. Keep this metaphor in mind if you're currently out of work; it will be little more than a passing blister in the flow of your life, soon to be replaced with a tough callous.

A s you consider changes you need to make, don't overreact and try to do everything at once. As the folks at AA like to say, one day at a time.

Y ou can tell a person's character best when he or she is under pressure. How are you holding up?

I f you're laid off, ask your (former) boss for help in making calls on your behalf, circulating your resume and referring you to other potential contacts, in addition to providing a positive recommendation.

Some aspirations . . . mean more to us, and we may never get over our failure to fulfill them. Psychiatrists may say that giving up part of our lives should cause mourning over the loss. This may indeed happen during transition, and may last longer than that in some cases. But the more likely emotion is joy at finally ridding ourselves of hopes that have turned heavy with disappointment. In the end it's relief, not grief, we feel as we relax into a state of lowered ambition.

Gilbert Brim, *Ambition: How We Manage Success and Failure throughout Our Lives*

I f a friend or colleague is axed, call and ask if you can help by circulating his or her resume, mentioning his or her situation to others or just being an emotional source of support. Someday that help will return to you in a way you cannot predict.

A ppreciate the laws of adversity:

Without adversity, there's no personal growth.

Adversity prepares us for bigger challenges and accomplishments.

Adversity reminds us how short our time on earth is, and how important it is to use wisely.

Adversity always contains hidden opportunities.

It's always darkest and coldest before the dawn.

Adversity forces us to adapt and change.

Adversity helps us find an inner reservoir of strength and courage, and surmounting it builds self-esteem and self-confidence.

As Job learned in the Old Testament, adversity helps build faith.

Adversity provides great stories for the grandchildren.

Adversity is a silent teacher. It's up to us to probe for its lessons.

If you lose a job after age 40, read about people whose greatest successes occurred after midlife, such as Gail Borden (inventor of condensed milk), Ray Kroc, Abraham Lincoln, Harry Truman and Colonel Sanders.

Be cynical. Look for a connection between what an outplacement firm recommends . . . and what their involvement in it costs them.

John Lucht, *Rights of Passage at $100,000 +*

Following are some things to keep in mind if you're working with an outplacement counselor:

1. The more aware you are up front of what you want out of the process, the more likely you are to get it.

2. Be aggressive and demanding of time and resources, but be reasonable and realistic in your demands and expectations.

3. Be clear in your mind about what an outplacement counselor can and will do and cannot or won't do for you.

4. You'll get out of it what you put into it, so go at it full tilt: do all the exercises; participate in the groups; think and act positively.

5. If you're married, get your spouse involved in the process.

6. If you need special help (for example, consultation on entrepreneurship or job search with a disability), ask for it.

7. Make deliberate changes from the recommended formats for cover letters, resumes and interview techniques.

8. Let your outplacement counselor be your point of catharsis, so that you don't take your anger out on family, friends or interviewers. Make sure you trust your counselor. If you don't, find someone else in the office.

9. Study their previous success stories.

10. Share your story with others, but don't be a complainer.

11. Ask lots of questions.

12. Don't wait for them to do it for you.

There's nothing you've misplaced or lost.
You've simply grown, you've faced the cost,
You've taken risks in being your best friend.
And I will be no further than
Each bold new step on unseen land;
I know the joy of watching your fears end.

Doug Peters, from the song *You're (Tough As) Nails*

"It's very nice, sweetheart, but you know you're not supposed to fax daddy at the office."

13
Going It
On Your Own

*One of the most powerful trends these days is the incredible
growth of self-employment, fueled primarily by people who run
home-based businesses. Indeed, entrepreneurship and selling
will be the two most important skills of the twenty-first century,
whether you work for yourself or someone else. There are many
sources of information and inspiration for would-be
entrepreneurs, and if you don't think you have what it takes to
be an entrepreneur or to sell, think again. Speak with people
who are doing it. If you start small and incrementally, perhaps
by turning a hobby into a business, you may be surprised at how
good you can become and the fast pace at which you achieve
results.*

*In the past 25 years I have found it mindboggling to discover how
many people start a new business, at home or elsewhere, without
ever going to talk to anybody else in the same kind of business.*

Richard Nelson Bolles, *What Color is Your Parachute?*

In recent years, millions of Americans have left corporate suites
and factory floors to go into business for themselves. They do it

for a variety of reasons, including the opportunity to have greater control over their time, the potential of significant financial reward and being able to have more fulfilling work. Perhaps this is the time to ask yourself what, other than a paycheck, you want from work, and whether now is the time to consider striking out on your own.

The difference between being self-employed and unemployed is having paying customers. What can you *do* that other people will pay you for doing? If your answer to that question is "middle management," then you desperately need to develop a new skill set.

Read Ralph Waldo Emerson's famous essay "Self-Reliance." This is timeless wisdom for anyone starting a business.

Read Wilson Harrell's column on the back page of *Success* magazine each month, and his book *For Entrepreneurs Only.*

Futurist Dan Burrus, author of the book *Technotrends,* believes that within the next seven years, close to half of all jobs will be newly created, and that many of the jobs that exist today will be gone.

While pessimistic futurists focus on the job-destroying power of technology, Burrus is more excited about its job-creating power. You don't have to be a scientist or a technologist to capitalize on this, he says, just as you don't need to know the physics of a telephone to make a call. People who get ahead in the new economy will be those who are able to find creative uses for new technologies.

"We can all learn new skills and develop a new mind-set," Burrus says. "Our ability to unlearn old skills and attitudes may be more important than our ability to learn new ones."

Martin Groder, MD, is a psychiatrist in private practice in Chapel Hill, North Carolina, who also does business consulting. He speaks of middle-aged Americans who intuitively know that they aren't really productively adding to society by attending meetings, shuffling paper and talking on the telephone. Groder tells of one client who worked as the head of a small division of a Fortune 500 corporation and spent half his time complaining about the parent company. After his job was eliminated, he spent a number of years working for other companies before finally starting his own business, which has become very successful. Now, he says, he's making a real difference.

Becky Jones, head of a Toronto career services firm bearing her name, worked with a human resources director who was outplaced and decided to start his own consulting business. She reports that the most difficult aspect for him to learn was the uneven pace of work and income. Though he initially experienced frequent mood swings and depression, by learning how to network and develop strategic alliances, he was able to stay active and build certainty into his business. Within two years, his income had risen almost 50 percent.

When Ian Simpson lost his position with a major investment firm, he used the opportunity to pursue the long-held dream of writing a book on mutual funds. In short order, he was commissioned to complete two more books. This led to extensive speaking engagements, and development of his own consulting practice.

When Dan Keeting lost his job of 26 years with a Toronto manufacturing company, he told his outplacement counselor, seemingly in jest, that his ideal job would include his two loves—the theater and travel. After deciding that he didn't want to work for another corporation, Keeting took acting classes and sought work as an extra. He conducted an extensive campaign of cold calls to obtain information and leads about commercials, movies and television work. He also developed a training program on travel to be conducted at a local college. He has been able to transfer his marketing and sales skills into his own new business—dealing with theater and travel.

Sometimes, it's necessary to let go of plans that seem attractive but would exact an exorbitant price. Sarah Smith's accounting position at a major U.S. manufacturer was eliminated as part of a major corporate restructuring in 1993. Smith worked with a friend to develop a business plan for a small retail store, but eventually concluded that its time demands would interfere with her priority of having more time with her new child. Ultimately, she decided to earn a teaching certificate and pursue work as a teacher, giving her more time flexibility.

Unless you're willing to take risks, you'll suffer paralyzing inhibitions, and you'll never know what you're capable of doing. Mistakes—missteps—are necessary for actualizing your vision, and necessary steps toward success.

Warren Bennis, *On Becoming a Leader*

The biggest challenge that many entrepreneurs face in making the transition from corporate life is mental. They need to change from a task-and-time orientation to a goal-and-output orientation. When you're an entrepreneur, nobody cares how many things are scratched off of your to-do list or how many hours you work.

Entrepreneur Dave Bruno says one of the hardest lessons for him to learn was that he had to be able to receive as well as give. Early in the startup of his business, he felt compelled to give away his products, thinking he was building market share. Fortunately, one early customer insisted upon paying full price, admonishing Bruno to start learning how to receive before he ran out of things to give.

When Barry Rein left the chemical industry after a 22-year career in management and purchased a bed-and-breakfast inn, he had to learn everything about the business, from gourmet cooking to finding craftspeople who could rennovate. It turned out to be far more demanding and frightening than he ever thought it would be. Nonetheless, after several years, he hasn't regretted his decision.

Here are 10 demographic groups that, if you target them and have good ideas, will make you wealthy:

1. Aging baby boomers.

2. The growing singles market.

3. New grandparents.

4. The sandwich generation.

5. Divorced women.

6. Purchasers of small luxury homes.

7. Vacation travelers.

8. Generation X.

9. Temporary and contract workers.

10. Home-based businesspeople.

Note that there's significant overlap between these groups (aging boomers are new grandparents and moving into smaller luxury homes as their children leave the nest). Note also that some trends straddle others (Generation X and divorced women both contribute to the growing singles market). Where multiple trends collide, look for opportunity; it's there!

Sometimes following your heart into an entrepreneurial venture requires giving yourself permission to dismiss what other people think. Tom Nolan spent 33 years as a product marketing manager with IBM Corp. before deciding to enroll in the Paperhanging Institute in Fairfield, New Jersey. Though he doesn't have a prestigious job anymore, when he wants to take a week off, he simply tells prospective customers that he's booked for the week.

There are many books that offer self-administered tests you can take to determine whether you've got what it takes to make it as an entrepreneur. One of the best was developed by the late Eugene Raudsepp, and is included in the reprint *Entrepreneurial Options; Best of the National Business Employment Weekly* (available by calling 800-JOB-HUNT). Raudsepp summarized the following traits that are essential to being a successful entrepreneur:

▶ A high motivation for achievement.

▶ An action orientation.

▶ A solid grasp on reality, with no wishful thinking, and a willingness to admit when you're having problems.

▶ Highly self-reliant, and not discouraged by external events.

▶ Self-confidence that's based in a belief in yourself and your ability to master challenges, bounce back from defeat and achieve goals.

▶ Always on the lookout for opportunities.

▶ Moderate, not significant, risk-taking.

▶ High motivation, incredible energy and "an infinite capacity for hard work."

▶ Patience and a long-term perspective.

▶ Persistence and tenacity.

▶ An ability to accept and learn from failure.

▶ A willingness to solve problems by understanding facts, analyzing different approaches and testing hypotheses before taking action.

The quiz included in Raudsepp's article can "help you decide if you've got the psychological characteristics to succeed in an entrepreneurial enterprise," he wrote.

Mary Anne van Arsdale, director of a small-business development center in Pennsylvania, describes the following 10 myths of entrepreneurship:

1. The best time to start a business is after a job search has stalled. In reality, the best time is while you're still employed, or immediately after termination, when the family's financial and emotional resources are still strong.

2. If you've got a good idea, a business will somehow grow around it.

3. Seeing entrepreneurship as a quick way to recover from job loss, without recognizing a significant investment that must be made before you begin to make progress.

4. Believing that you'll be your own boss (others will always play a role).

5. Seeing entrepreneurship as an easy way to regain self-respect.

6. Believing you can get rich quick with minimal risk.

7. Believing you can do something better than anyone else.

8. Thinking that if you can manage someone else's business, you can manage your own.

9. Believing that you'll have more time for your family.

10. Believing that you'll have more security.

Once you've gone through the mid-life transition satisfactorily, faced mortality and forged a new life system, this stage [47 to 54] might feel like the best time of life.

Janet Hagberg and Richard Leider, *The Inventurers:*
Excursions in Life and Career Renewal

In his book, *Growing a Business,* Paul Hawken warns against inadvertently starting more than one business at a time, a common cause of failure among startups. Someone who self-publishes a book, for example, must realize that he or she is actually starting three businesses: writing, publishing and promotion. Each of the three may require different skills.

Steven C. Brandt, in his book *Entrepreneuring: The Ten Commandments for Building a Growth Company,* describes three related occupational hazards faced by entrepreneurs. First, they tend to be more concerned about what they have to sell than what their potential customers want to buy. Second, they tend to generalize about who their customers are, without applying disciplined thinking as to which specific segments of the market might buy from them. Third, because of their enthusiasm and optimism, they sometimes fail to specify precise reasons why someone might want to buy what they're selling. "Because it's better," Brandt says, "is not sufficiently precise."

John Thomas, an executive recruiter with Ward Howell International in Chicago found that 60 percent of executives who left Procter & Gamble to start new businesses didn't survive two years.

The main reason, he found, was that they were too accustomed to having staff support. Ask yourself: Can you cook and wash dishes as well as crunch numbers?

Appreciate the stress that might be involved in running your own business. Jim Kacena left the corporate world to become an entrepreneur. He started a hardware store, and did well, but the store increasingly dominated every second of his waking time. He ended up in the hospital for heart surgery, with a failed marriage. While in the hospital, he decided he had to change. Via networking, he came into contact with the career outplacement field. Finding that he missed working in the corporate arena, and using his psychology background, he has worked in the field for the past 15 years. Now working as an outplacement counselor, Kacena says the combination of his life experiences make him ideal for the job.

Sometimes, trying to help others can result in a successful business. Lane Nemeth founded Discover Toys, Inc. after being frustrated that the educational toys available to children at the daycare center where she was an administrator couldn't be purchased by parents. She wanted for her own children what was available to daycare students. This was the impetus for her creating a business selling top-quality toys to parents in their homes. Today, Discover Toys is a $93 million business.

Seeing unmet needs around the office where you work can also be the genesis of a successful business. Robert W. Horgan asked himself why there wasn't computer software to maximize revenue in the highest profit center of the hotel where he was a manager: group sales and catering. Two years later, he started Newmarket Software Systems Inc. to do just that. Today, he owns a $12 million business.

Fresh out of high school, Forrest Ridgway bought a small bike shop. Today, his two Bike World stores dominate the market in Des Moines, Iowa, and are among the top 100 in the country. His most important action in the early days was to invest every extra nickel in the business. He was used to having no money, so didn't miss it.

Jan Finkelstein had recently been promoted to vice president of a large teaching hospital, when the entire top management team turned over within a few months. In short order, her promotion was rescinded, and her responsibilities diminished. She spent every spare minute of the next year daydreaming, thinking, planning, asking for help and networking. This resulted in the design of a business to link corporate and nonprofit organizations for the pursuit of mutually beneficial goals. Still, she didn't quit her job until she had enough business lined up to generate nearly one-year's cash flow. Her largest customer was her former employer. "I'm convinced that the most important thing I did was to design my own future and sell it, market it and push it to make it happen."

In his book, *Innovation and Entrepreneurship,* Peter F. Drucker outlines the do's, the don'ts, and the conditions of effective innovation.

The Do's

1. Begin with an analysis of opportunities, not of what you want to sell.

2. Go out and look, ask questions and listen. Use both the right and left sides of your brain, because innovation is both conceptual and perceptual.

3. Effective innovation must be simple and focused. If it does more than one thing, it confuses.

4. Effective innovations start small.

5. Successful innovation aims at leadership from the very beginning.

The Don'ts

1. Don't try to be clever.

2. Don't diversify or try to do too many things at once.

3. Don't try to innovate for the future, but instead, innovate for the present.

The Conditions

1. Innovation requires knowledge, ingenuity and hard work.

2. Successful innovators must build upon their strengths.

3. Effective innovation must always be close to the market, focused on the market and completely market-driven.

Many writers agree that getting your name into print, as tough as it may be, is easy compared with keeping your name in print. Selling your product off the shelves is the real creative challenge.

Martin Yate, *Beat the Odds*

FREELANCING

If you have talents for which others will pay you, freelancing is a good way to make extra money, learn business skills and perhaps develop a full-time venture. Broadly defined, freelancing can be anything: writing, photography, carpentry, accounting, sales management, babysitting, any work for which you charge others on an hourly or project basis, but typically without having established a corporate organization.

Claire Braz-Valentine left an administrator's job at the University of California Santa Cruz to follow her heart and become a writer after taking early retirement at age 50. It took her almost a year to get used to having so much "free time," and to give herself permission to enjoy writing in the morning and reading in the afternoon. At that point, she was able to begin building a successful business.

Ed Myers is a freelance writer and author of *When Parents Die: A Guide for Adults.* He's been writing since the early 1980s, and readily acknowledges that freelancing is a tough way to make a living. But if you've got an insatiable curiosity and love to write, it gives you great freedom. Myers' advice for freelance writers can apply across the board to all freelancers:

1. Start with simple things you can pull off and build from your strengths.

2. Branch out from that solid foundation.

3. Get and stay organized; once you start freelancing, it's not a hobby anymore, it's a business. Learn about finance, technology, filing systems and everything else you need to know to run a business so that you don't waste time on administrative details when you should be working.

4. Keep your overhead low and take a long view financially.

5. Be responsible about protecting yourself with health and disability insurance.

6. Find professional companionship, such as a writer's association or an Internet group.

7. Find partners who can help in your work, such as an editor or agent.

8. Diversify your interests.

9. Keep your sense of humor.

10. Understand that freelancing is a lonely profession, and take steps to keep yourself connected with the rest of the world.

L ook for spin-offs so that you can leverage the value of your work. Gary Trudeau recycles cartoons into calendars and coffee mugs. Jay Conrad Levinson has built a successful seminar business around his "Guerrilla Marketing" books. How can you make your work do double duty?

S ometimes you can use a small springboard to take a giant leap. Martin Yate was turned down by 64 publishers before his career book *Knock 'Em Dead* was accepted by Bob Adams Press. Yate received an advance of only $100. Today, the book has sold more than two million copies. Perhaps more important, it made it much easier for Yate to get his subsequent books published.

I f you have specialized knowledge in an area, or even if you don't but have a strong interest and willingness to learn, creating a newsletter can be an enjoyable and lucrative form of freelancing. Two good resources are:

Newsletter on Newsletters	914-876-2081
Newsletter Publishers Association	800-356-9302

R obin Alden was working as a journalist and became fascinated with the economic and environmental controversies surrounding fishing along her beloved Maine coast. She started the *Commercial Fisheries News* newsletter as a way of trying to get people talking (instead of screaming) with one another. Her newsletter has become the most credible source of information on the New England fishing industry, and she has since started two others.

When 34-year-old Andrew Smith lost his job with a Wall Street firm, he decided to become a corporate turnaround specialist. Because he had no experience, he started a newsletter in order to develop credibility. Working with Barbara Barra of the New York office of Lee Hecht Harrison Inc., Smith produced the newsletter, including interviews with experts in the field, and purchased a mailing list. To promote the newsletter, he looked for every opportunity for exposure. The publication lasted three years before stopping because Smith's new job with a turnaround firm became too time-consuming.

British writer Andrew Crofts began his book, *How to Make Money from Freelance Writing,* with a quotation by Samuel Johnson from 1776: "No man but a blockhead ever wrote, except for money." No matter how much you love writing, Crofts says, unless you learn how to sell your writing, you'll eventually become disillusioned and give up trying. Besides, Crofts says, "the possibility of hunger is a great motivator."

Value is now created by 'productivity' and 'innovation,' both applications of knowledge to work.

Peter F. Drucker, *Post-Capitalist Society*

With advances in desktop publishing technology and a growing numbers of printers used to working with self-publishers, publishing your own book is now well within the realm of possibility. The two best resources for anyone interested in self-publishing are:

▶ *The Self-Publishing Manual* by Dan Poynter.

▶ *The Complete Guide to Self-Publishing* by Tom and Marilyn Ross.

Once you've decided to publish your own book, get a copy of *1001 Ways to Market Your Books* by John Kremer. Though this book is primarily intended for those who have published or plan to publish multiple titles, there are great ideas for authors and single book publishers.

If you're comfortable in front of groups of people, have a good sense of humor, a powerful message and have experience as a public speaker, consider the world of paid speaking. Two of the best reference books on the subject are *Speak and Grow Rich,* by Dottie and Lilly Walters, and *How to Make It Big in the Seminar Business* by Paul Karasik.

Writing and speaking are highly complementary activities. Many speakers sell hundreds of books in conjunction with giving talks. Such writers as Wayne Dyer, Leo Buscaglia and James Redfield became best-selling authors on the basis of their aggressive development of speaking opportunities.

Before you can start charging for speeches, you'll probably have to give many—perhaps hundreds—of "freebies." Local service groups, such as Rotary, Kiwanis, Lions and Optimist Clubs, have an insatiable appetite for speakers.

In his book, *Swim with the Sharks Without Being Eaten Alive,* Harvey McKay, who is one of the nation's most highly paid speakers, describes 11 ways to win over your audience:

1. Know why the group invited you to speak, and how your talk was publicized and positioned for the audience.

2. Understand the group's purpose.

3. Understand the group's characteristics (professional, social, demographic, career level and so on).

4. Find out who recent speakers were, how they were received, and try to get copies of their remarks.

5. Find out who the most successful past speakers were and what made them successful.

6. Find out how to personalize your speech for the group, including using appropriate humor and avoiding taboo topics.

7. Try to speak with opinion leaders in the group beforehand.

8. Find out who will introduce you, how you'll be positioned and what nice things you can say about him or her.

9. Anticipate tough questions.

10. Ascertain which messages will provide genuine "take-home" value for the group, and whether take-home materials are appropriate.

11. Find a group "insider" who can help you develop the speech and give you reliable feedback on your performance.

Join a Toastmasters International group in your area, and if there's not one available, start one.

If you're serious about a speaking career, which means you've taken the advice presented thus far, you enjoy speaking and are willing to travel, and believe that people will pay to hear you speak, consider subscribing to Burt Dubin's Speaking Success System. There's no better way to quickly learn about the structure and dynamics of the professional speaking business. It won't take many paid speeches to offset the cost. This resource and the consulting services that come with it are incredible confidence builders. For more information, contact Speaking Success System at 800-321-1225 or online at BDUBINSPKR@aol.com.

If you decide to freelance, take it seriously. William Kutick spent two decades in journalism before starting a one-man marketing consultancy after having been laid off or fired eight times, including four times from failed startup companies. He resolved to take charge of his fate, and now writes ads, annual reports, speeches and direct-mail pieces for corporate clients. "Once I decided this was a business, not freelancing, I got really successful really fast," he says.

This year alone will probably see 10 million new people join the online marketplace. Every week, hundreds of entrepreneurs will increase the ranks of your competition.

Jay Conrad Levinson and Charles Rubin,
Guerrilla Marketing Online

Knowing up front whether you're creating a business in which you plan to have a long-term involvement, or that you hope to build and sell, will profoundly affect the way it's structured and financed.

If your plan is to build and sell the company, read the book *Ultrapreneuring: Taking a Venture from Start-Up to Harvest in Three Years or Less* by James B. Arkebauer. This tough-minded book will outline the kind of people, planning, financing, marketing and cash management that's required if you aspire to grab the brass ring.

⬧⬧⬧

Do what you love, and the money will follow. Much has been written about the provocative title of Marsha Sinetar's book. While it may work out that way, for the fledgling entrepreneur, a more honest truism might be: Do what you fear and the money will follow.

If you are a woman starting a business, do these two things. First read Jane Wessman's book *Dive Right In, the Sharks Won't Bite*. Second, contact the National Association of Women Business Owners (NAWBO) in Chicago at 312-922-0465.

Industrial engineer your daily processes. The entrepreneur's most valuable asset is time. Bring in the ghost of Frederick Taylor to make sure you're using yours as effectively as possible.

If you've been punching a clock for most of your career either literally or figuratively, leave it at the door when you start your own business.

CONSULTING

"Everyone thinks they can be a consultant," says career and organizational expert Joan Lloyd of Milwaukee. "The old adage is still right, however: don't quit your day job." Lloyd speaks from experience. When she decided to leave the corporate world and pursue a career in training and development, she couldn't get hired because she had no business experience. She created her own experience by teaching evening and weekend courses, which eventually gave her entree to working with larger corporations. She started her newspaper column in the early 1980s, and as readership expanded, that led to speaking engagements, which in turn led to a television program. Through it all, she worked a regular job, which she didn't quit until she was offered a contract to write the book *The Career Decisions Planner.*

The first thing to do if you plan to pursue a consulting career is to get your rolodex in shape. If you have not already taken the advice (from the chapter on Networking) to install ACT! on your computer, or some similar form of contact-management system, this is the time to do it.

If you plan to start a consulting practice, rather than beginning with what you know, start with what potential clients need to know. Make sure that there's a market for your services before you invest in four-color glossy brochures.

Consulting is a business, so develop a business plan. Mike Florimbi, president of Florimbi Partners International, a Dallas-based firm specializing in international development for U.S. corporations, says his consulting practice grew from concept to successful venture as a result of a well-targeted, well-executed marketing plan.

Successful consultants bring two things to their clients: technical knowledge and process skills. The most secure business will be based on a solid combination of the two. There are, for example, many consulting firms that assist corporations in implementing programs, such as total quality management. They must understand both the statistical and management processes involved, but in many cases, it's more important that they understand the human and organizational dimension of change in order to successfully implement a program.

Philadelphia career consultant Douglas B. Richardson has built a successful career counseling business by simultaneously generalizing and specializing. He provides a broad range of career counseling, corporate consulting and training services to a variety of clients. At the same time, his background as a practicing attorney has enabled him to develop a strong niche with lawyers who are seeking career changes.

As a consultant, all you've got to sell is your time. Consider supplementing that with tangible products. Randi Levitz and Lee Noel started a business providing consulting to colleges and universities in areas related to student retention. The more they traveled, the more apparent it became that there were opportunities to grow the business by developing training programs, computer software and other products that could supplement their consulting practice. By doing this, they were able to smooth out cash flow and reduce the company's dependence on their time. More important, they were able to generate capital to finance its growth to over 70 staff members. They recently sold the business to USA Group of Indianapolis, and have stayed on to help see USA Group/Noel-Levitz into the next phase of development.

In a consulting practice, it's typically better to have a few large clients than many small clients. Michel Robert is president of Decision Processes International, and author of the book *The Strategist CEO: How Visionary Executives Build Organizations*. Robert has created a $4 million worldwide training business by developing collaborative partnerships with a limited number of clients for whom he provides extensive work.

The most important outcome of any consulting engagement isn't a fee, and it's not a final report. It's a relationship. Successful consultants use every opportunity to build ongoing relationships with their clients.

Build the habit of doing something every day that contributes moving you from employee to entrepreneur, and be ruthless about how your time is spent. Especially at the beginning, you must jealously guard your time and be certain that you are not spending it in ways that are counterproductive.

Barbara J. Winter, *Making a Living Without a Job*

If your plan is to develop a substantial business, rather than simply meet your cash flow needs through consulting work, don't take another step without reading the book *Million Dollar Consulting: The Professional's Guide to Growing a Practice* by Alan Weiss. Here's a key point to keep in mind if you're in it for the long term:

The best, longest-lived most rewarding client relationships are those based on conceptual agreement of what is to be accomplished. The 'how' is subordinated to the end result.

In a *National Business Employment Weekly* article, Houda E. Samaha, founder of Innovation Management, a Cambridge, Massachusetts, consulting firm, outlined the following six pitfalls to avoid as a new consultant:

▶ Not knowing your client's business; focusing on symptoms, but not diagnosing the fundamental problems.

▶ Being arrogant or condescending.

▶ Having a narrow focus and not seeing the big picture.

▶ Not solidifying up-front agreements concerning the project price, purpose, scope and duration, deliverables, progress-tracking and deadlines.

▶ Promising more than you can deliver.

▶ Inadequate follow-up.

Ivan Levison started a home-based business providing freelance copywriting support to high-technology companies 17 years ago. He was, as he says, a refugee from the corporate world. His business has been very successful. The key factor has been his definition of a niche and ruthless focus. "You can't be a mile wide and an inch deep," he says. "You have to be like an ice skater, pressing your entire weight down upon a very precise target area." To see Levison's homepage on the World Wide Web, link to: http://www.levison.com.

The day you sign your first client, you should have a pretty good idea of who the next three or four clients will be. The day you start your first project with a client, you should have a pretty good idea of what the second project will be with that client.

Whenever you finish a project with a client, ask these three questions:

1. What could I have done better?

2. What should I do next?

3. Who else could benefit from having me work with them?

If you're serious about being a consultant, join the Institute of Management Consultants (212-697-9693) and pursue certification. The Institute publishes the *Journal of Management Consulting*.

A ccording to Mary Cronin, a professor of management at Boston College and author of the book, *Doing Business on the Internet,* the Net will provide enormous new opportunities for small consulting firms. One- and two-person operations that could never have afforded marketing to large corporations now have a vehicle for doing so.

Telecommunications is the driving force that is simultaneously creating the huge global economy and making its parts smaller and more powerful.

John Naisbitt, *Global Paradox*

STARTING YOUR OWN BUSINESS

D on't let horror stories about the number of small business failures scare you off. Many small companies that fail do so because they aren't backed by a strong commitment from the owner.

D on't start a business as a way of avoiding a job search. As anyone who's self-employed will tell you, to run your own business is to be in a job-search mode every day.

Y ou have to survive before you can succeed. If you start a new business, don't be like the wide receiver who fumbles the ball because he's eyeing the end zone before he's secured the catch.

S cott Shaw opened the Austin Grill Restaurant in Washington, DC, in 1987, and its Tex-Mex format was immediately successful. Several more were opened in succeeding years. In 1993, he opened a restaurant in Boca Raton, Florida, near where a Chi Chi's Restaurant had failed earlier. The partners rationalized away the earlier failure, but as their own restaurant began to sink, they learned "the awful truth that the worst case can always get even worse."

Shaw says they failed because they didn't know the market and failed to develop an appropriate strategy for it. They closed the restaurant before its losses could jeopardize the rest of the company. He now offers this "million-dollar" advice: "Take care of the downside and the upside will take care of itself."

Sometimes, successfully starting a new business means letting go of work you love. Joe Wolf loved labor relations. So when he started his own firm—Human Resources Management Corp. in St. Louis—it seemed like a natural to include labor relations along with outplacement and career planning as services offered to corporate clients. Wolf found, however, that labor relations work interfered with the time required for his other businesses, and prevented him from effectively marketing. He had to let go of that practice in the interest of the larger business.

In starting a new venture, it's important to listen to your troubles. James C. Collins and Jerry L. Porras of the Stanford Graduate School of Business found in their book *Built to Last: Success Habits of Visionary Companies* that successful companies often don't have much success early on. The initial difficulties and frustrations, though, force them to think through exactly what it is they're trying to accomplish—their true mission. This process helps them develop a broader and longer-term perspective.

Developing new uses for technology can be the springboard for launching a new business. James Gonyea was one of thousands of people who made a living advising others on their careers—one person at a time. Then he became intrigued with the possibility of giving career counseling online. He connected with America Online to develop an electronic career center. He also wrote a book on the subject of electronic job search. By being first onboard, or rather online, Gonyea was able to make a quantum leap. Today, Gonyea & Associates is 15 to 20 times larger than it was when he was dealing with clients individually.

Starting a business can feel like the loneliest experience in the world. Alison Davis left her position as director of the Public Management Program at the Stanford Graduate School of Business to start a business of her own. The MBA Non-Profit Connection created summer internships for MBA students with nonprofit organizations. Her biggest problem in the first year has been loneliness. She copes by inviting friends out for coffee and lunch breaks.

Take the advice of Napoleon Hill in his book, *Think and Grow Rich,* and create a "mastermind" of experts and mentors to advise you on your business.

Find an experienced entrepreneur to serve as a mentor. When Helene and Bobby Stone started their own business after Bobby lost his job, they asked for advice from a friend, Norm Brodsky, a successful entrepreneur. The two most important lessons he taught them were to preserve capital and go after high-margin business. But in terms of making the transition from employee to entrepreneur, for Bobby it was the realization that he had to transcend his old salesman mentality (all sales are good, short-term targets) and blend it with a businessman's mentality (making sure that all sales support the long-term viability of the business).

David Powell, a Woodside, California, executive recruiter specializing in small, high-growth companies, says "there are guys we've put in startups that failed, while others have made double-digit millions in personal wealth." Have a goal bigger than making a ton of money and you're less likely to be disappointed.

The entrepreneur must think emotionally on the upside and rationally on the downside. Let your dreams soar in the clouds, but keep your intellect firmly rooted in the realities of the present.

[The] Fatal Assumption is: if you understand the technical work of a business, you understand a business that does that technical work. And the reason it's fatal is that it just isn't true. In fact, it's the root cause of most business failures!

Michael E. Gerber, *The E Myth: Why Most Small Businesses Don't Work and What to Do about It*

Sometimes, you just want to show them! In 1985, Ian Leopold was a senior at Hobart College in Geneva, New York, and president of the entrepreneur's club. As a school project, he completed the business plan for a shopping guide in which local merchants would purchase advertising to reach students. He was flunked by his professor. He set out to prove the professor wrong, and today his Campus Concepts company is a nationwide, multimillion dollar business.

Love your product. Sally G. Norodick is a 50-year-old former banker who founded Edmark Corp. in Redmond, Washington. The company produces educational computer software, and Norodick reviews every program personally to make sure it's fun as well as educational.

Anne Robinson, co-founder of Windham Hill Records, gives this advice to any world-be entrepreneur: Stay focused and grow incrementally. It's as important, she says, to take care of what you have as it is to look for new opportunities. As soon as you're successful, competitors will attack. If your attention is somewhere else, you're likely to fail.

To be an effective entrepreneur, you need to learn how to cost-effectively promote your product. One of the best ways to generate ideas is to read the *Guerrilla Marketing* line of books by Jay Conrad Levinson.

Zachary P. Koczanski is owner of Anazak Productions, an independent producer of audio and video programs. He left the corporate world in 1985 and spent part of every day on the phone trying to find new customers or to increase his business from current customers. Several years ago, he began doing a great deal of work with several large pharmaceutical corporations.

"I got fat, dumb and happy," he says. But because of the health care cost squeeze, that business disappeared and he "really had to scramble." He now knows not to rest on his laurels, but also knows that having once achieved that success, he won't rest until he has done it again.

It's important to know when to bail out of an entrepreneurial venture. Dr. Martin Groder tells of a woman in her mid-30s with an accounting management background who was let go by the local branch of a multinational corporation. She decided to set up her own business providing financial services for "money-challenged" individuals. Unfortunately, she didn't anticipate the significant emotional needs of her clientele, which drained her of time, money and energy. Eventually, she moved back to her home state, got a job with an established company and is now very happy.

S pend more than you think you can afford on business cards, brochures and other promotional materials that give your business its identity. Marti Hess owns Cygnet Studios, an art and music business in Elizabethtown, Pennsylvania. She uses products from specialty paper companies, desktop publishing software and clip art to economically produce colorful brochures that can convey a big company image at a small company price.

N ever buy equipment you don't really need just because you think it will give you a nice tax write-off.

The real lesson here may not be that people are expendable to large corporations, but that the large corporation itself is becoming irrelevant to people who want more from their work than a paycheck.

George Gendron, Editor-in-Chief of *Inc. Magazine*

FRANCHISING

D rake Beam Morin outplacement counselors give psychological tests to unemployed executives. Those who wish to start their own businesses, but don't have the profile of an independent operator, are urged to buy a franchise rather than start something from scratch, the firm reports.

C hicago outplacement counselor Jim Kacena worked with an individual who used franchising to put it all together. He had been in corporate finance for many years when his job was eliminated. He did much soul-searching and decided he'd always wanted to teach; he also had a strong interest in computers. He bought a franchise from a company that teaches computer skills to preschool and kindergarten-age children. His business skills allowed him to successfully manage the operation, his love of computers let him meet his vocational interests and he got fulfillment from working with the children.

If you're considering a franchise, read about it carefully. Be cautious of various ranking systems, including those of *Inc.* and *Success* magazines, which have so many categories, many companies can claim to be first in their category (yet there's no ranking criteria).

Every year, the *National Business Employment Weekly* asks industry insiders for their evaluations. Their assessments are based on reports from happy franchisees, a good reputation, solid growth experience, fair contracts for franchisees, money-making potential, the availability of good locations and superior management. To order a copy of this annual report, call 800-730-1111, and request story #103.

Order the pamphlet "Are You Ready for Franchising?" from the Small Business Administration (SBA) by calling 202-205-6780. Also request a publications list from the International Franchise Association in Washington DC at 202-628-8000.

If a franchiser offers to sell you a franchise without thoroughly checking you out, put your hand on your wallet and run away as fast as you can.

Ellen Shubart, editor of *Franchise Buyer* magazine, says that buying a franchise is statistically much safer than starting your own business, but advises would-be franchisees to watch for the following pitfalls:

▶ Contract language that favors franchisers over franchisees.

▶ A franchise system that is past its prime.

▶ Lack of flexibility offered to franchisees in operations.

▶ Renegade franchisees.

▶ A poorly developed franchisee training and support program.

▶ Encroachment by other franchisees or the franchiser, or limited territories.

▶ Undercapitalization and poor cash management.

A s you evaluate opportunities, read the *Uniform Franchise Offering Circular,* which the franchise company is legally obligated to provide to you at least 10 days before you sign a franchise contract. Unless you're certain you understand every word, review it with a lawyer knowledgeable in franchise law (to obtain the latest edition of the *Directory of Franchise Attorneys,* call 800-289-4232).

B e prepared to work your tail off. When San Francisco attorney Victor Aron and his wife Lindy Edward, a nurse at the city jail, tired of their jobs, they bought a Body Shop retailing franchise. The workload was so overwhelming that they had to have Victor's mother come in from Chicago to help with the startup. Now, they say, business is going well, and they are considering opening a second store.

Go back to the drawing board; keep adding creativity until risk goes away. If it never goes, pass on the deal, no matter how good it looks.

Wilson Harrell, *For Entrepreneurs Only*

TEMPORARY WORK

According to Paul Hawkinson, editor of the *Fordyce Letter,* one of every two executives who works in a temporary position ends up being extended an offer of permanent employment.

Between 1990 and 1995, temporary and full-time employment agencies created 899,000 new jobs, more than any other sector of the economy.

Milwaukee-based Manpower Inc. reports global sales of more than $6 billion. It employs 10,000+ permanent staff members to oversee the temporary work of 1.5 million workers.

Craig Schrotenboer, vice president for people at Herman-Miller Inc., advises new graduates to consider temporary work as a way to start their careers. It's a great way to learn about different industries and try out different positions, he says.

David Naiditch, executive director of Dave Transportation, a Boston company that buses the disabled and hires many part-time professionals, offers the following recommendations for anyone considering temping:

1. Get to know the people who do the hiring.

2. Be ready to take unscheduled emergency work.

3. Stay within your level of competence.

4. Don't do it just for the money, do it because you love the work or the people you meet.

5. Develop a plan for how temping fits in with your overall career goals.

6. Invest all of the extra money you make.

For a nuts and bolts overview of temporary employment at the clerical, front line or middle management level, read *VGM's Guide to Temporary Employment* by Lewis R. Baratz. As Baratz points out, being a temp entails two job searches: first, passing the interview screens of the temporary help company; second, being assigned work once you're on board. This book includes practical advice on how to maximize your work hours, register with multiple companies, aggressively develop relationships and get along with the placement companies for which you work.

When James Nelson was released from his position as assistant vice president with a quasi-government institution in Minneapolis, he decided that after 18 years with the same organization, he wanted to pursue his interest and aptitude in accounting. He took evening courses to help prepare for the CPA exam, and worked through a temporary agency to obtain work at banks to accrue experience. Eventually, he saw an opening posted for a tax accountant to prepare trust tax returns and was hired for the job. He has since passed the CPA exam and been promoted.

Doing interim work during a period of unemployment can help build your self confidence. When John Thompson lost his position with a Toronto law firm, he entered a shared facility arrangement with several other lawyers to develop an independent practice. Meanwhile, he continued his search for a corporate position. As he told his outplacement counselor, he felt much more self-sufficient after a stint on his own.

For a complete roundup of firms nationwide that place executives and managers in interim positions, review the special report on professional temping produced by the *National Business Employment Weekly.* To order a copy of this report, call 800-730-1111, and request story #901.

Peter Daigle, an employment lawyer with Weir and Foulds in Toronto, suggests that an employment contract for temporary project work might cover the following key areas:

▶ Job duties, expectations of performance and authority, including how performance will be measured.

▶ Management rights to change job duties.

▶ The terms of the contract.

▶ Compensation, including base salary, pay raises (if any) and benefits (if any).

▶ An exclusive service clause specifying your work week for the employer, which the temporary worker will probably want to modify to have time for generating other contract work.

▶ A noncompetition or nonsolicitation clause, which—if it must be accepted—should be kept to as short a time period as possible so as not to restrict your ability to find work.

▶ A provision concerning confidential information, which also should not be so unreasonable as to limit your search for new work.

▶ A termination clause, including what grounds may be given for dismissal and required notice.

Daigle suggests having an employment law specialist review the contract, and says that some companies will actually pay for the review.

Gerry Calce lost his job as a distribution and logistics manager for a major Toronto food manufacturer and distributor when the company was sold. He was offered the option of continuing to work for the company on a six-month contract, which contained a two-week termination clause. Accepting the offer gave Calce a foundation for conducting a job search while continuing to have an income. He arranged his work schedule so that he could perform company work in his home office on weekends, giving him time for networking during the week. He also was able to negotiate other favorable changes in the contract originally presented to him by the employer.

As of this writing, the best way to plug your business into cyberspace is by reading the book *Guerrilla Marketing Online* by Jay Conrad Levinson and Charles Rubin. This book will show you how to use electronic mail, bulletin board services and electronic storefronts, and provides guerrilla strategies for making the most effective use of each. Levinson and Rubin emphasize that, to succeed, you must be aggressive and persevere.

Look for diamonds in the rough. Tom Hui was a computer consultant who, in 1984, developed a management program for a freestanding surgery center. As he watched the surgery center industry grow, he realized it would make an attractive market. He rewrote the program to make it more flexible so that it would appeal more broadly, and began to market it. He implemented 12 centers in his first year. By the end of 1996, he expects to have about 250 centers operating with his software.

Don't underestimate the competition, but neither let it scare you off. Mark Fuller wanted to open a fast-food restaurant in Mt. Vernon, Iowa, with his father-in-law. They didn't let the specter of McDonald's and Burger King scare them off. They picked a corner opposite Hardys and Pizza Hut to begin their

Banquet on a Bun (BOAB) restaurant. Combining Mark's expertise in full-service restaurants and Al's expertise in fast food, they created a restaurant with quick service but a higher quality menu than typical fast food. Now well into their second year, they've carved out a considerable niche, despite the fact that more fast-food restaurants are opening up on their corner of Highways 1 and 30.

Sometimes it pays to swim against the stream. Bill Tank was a senior vice president and chief credit officer for Norwest Bank in Des Moines, Iowa. At a time when Norwest was acquiring other banks as part of a larger national trend toward consolidation, Tank saw an opportunity to create a small specialty bank that would focus on building superior relationships with small- to medium-sized businesses. He left Norwest, and today is chief executive officer of First Business Bank of Iowa. In this, he is bringing to banking a trend that has proven successful for niche players in other industries experiencing consolidation, ranging from steel (mini-mills) to brewing (mini-breweries) to airlines (renewed success of regional carriers).

Arlynn Greenbaum was head of marketing at a major publishing firm when her job was eliminated in conjunction with a 1991 merger. In the back of her mind, she'd always thought there should be a speaker's bureau just for authors. Because of her contacts in the publishing industry, in her first year, she was able to recruit 150 authors, most of whom had their membership fee paid by their publishing companies. She now has more than 350 authors, and is not actively recruiting.

Be ready to be tough. When Roger Christian's retail photographic equipment business nosedived in the late 1980s, he had to slash expenses. He even used recycled envelopes for his out-mail. Today, business is booming, but the memories have prompted him to look at each expenditure with a hard eye.

Phyllis Levy loved her job as a product development and marketing specialist with Campbell Soups. She had been responsible for the successful introduction of Le Menu dinners and the turnaround of Prego. During the 1990s, however, the company's focus turned to cost-cutting and there was less money for the innovative projects upon which she thrived.

In early 1994, Levy left to start her own business, The OUTrepreneur Group. Now she provides new product development and marketing for companies that never had or have downsized away their "intrapreneurial" resources. She says that she took with her the exciting work she likes, and left behind that which wasn't fun or rewarding.

Synergy. Many people in the business and financial communities have given up hope that it ever occurs. Not, however, Linda Kline, Amy Friedman and Jaye Smith. They were, respectively, experts in executive search, outplacement, and education and development. After two years of research, they founded the Arbor Group Inc in New York City. Their businesses are mutually supportive, and they cross-sell for each other. Many of their clients, mostly Fortune 500 companies, use the group for all three services. As of this writing, the group is doubling the size of its office from 4,500 to 9,000 square feet. The key to their success has been careful strategic planning, and developing strategic alliances with other companies that provide related work in other parts of the country.

Sometimes you can use "ignorance" to your own advantage. Paul and Gary Giegerich bought a failing dart company in 1988. At the time, the firm's wholesale sales had fallen to $225,000. Because they didn't know the business, they came in with a fresh perspective and spent a great deal of time listening to customers and looking for market niches. Today, Dart Mart Inc., based in Manhattan, has more than $10 million in sales. More recently, they formed a partnership with comedian David Brenner and opened the Amsterdam Billiard Club in uptown Manhattan. The club has been packed since the day it opened.

But with more than 570,000 franchised units in the country, and some 42,000 starting up this year, franchisees can't afford the luxury of waiting for their corporate honchos to think them out of their latest competitive jam. Their very survival is at stake.

Jay Finegan, *Inc. Magazine.*

"He'll be fine, Miss Brentwood . . . I merely transferred power to him for a brief moment."

14
Serve and Share

The ultimate paradox of landing the job you want or moving ahead in the job you've got is that by helping others and sharing what you have, your own long-term career success and personal happiness will grow. As Confucius said some 2,500 years ago, the surest road to success is helping other people succeed. And as Chuang Tzu remarked several hundred years later, the surest way to be unhappy is to devote yourself exclusively to the pursuit of your own happiness.

Here is a test to find whether your mission on earth is finished: If you're alive, it isn't.

Richard Bach, *Illusions: The Adventures of a Reluctant Messiah*

How can a society that was founded on the basis of the individual's right to the pursuit of happiness have so many unhappy people? One reason might be that happiness is often defined in overly self-centered terms. More than 2,000 years ago, the Taoist philosopher Chuang Tzu said:

The ambitious run day and night in pursuit of honors, constantly in anguish about the success of their plans, dreading the miscalculation that may wreck everything. Thus, they are alienated from themselves, exhausting their real life in the service of the shadow created by their insatiable hope . . . . My opinion is that you never find happiness until you stop looking for it.

Doug Peters is pastor of the Solon United Methodist Church in Solon, Iowa. Ask him how he decided to become a minister and he'll tell you that it's a decision that's made on a daily basis. A talented folk singer and counselor, Peters has often thought about roads not traveled. His most compelling reason for not changing, however, is his continuous ability to make a difference in other people's lives, which he is quick to say makes an even bigger difference in his life. Recordings of Doug's music can be obtained through Paradox 21 Press at 800-644-3889.

You can have everything in life you want if you'll just help enough other people get what they want.

Zig Ziglar, *Ziglar on Selling*

In her book *Love Your Work and Success Will Follow,* Arlene S. Hirsch cites geroentological research showing that being open to new experiences is the single most important lifelong trait for successful living. If you're approaching retirement, she says, "the key is to involve yourself in the activities which you find stimulating, regardless of the financial payoff."

Read Ecclesiastes in the Bible, especially if you're dealing with the emotional turmoil of being at midlife and mid-career. As Harold Kushner says in his book *When All You've Ever Wanted Isn't Enough,* "No one else [in the Bible] shares his innermost fears and frustrations with us the way Ecclesiastes does." He had many observations on the role of work, including:

"A man can do nothing better than to eat and drink and find satisfaction with his work." (2:24)

"Two are better than one, because they have a good return for their work: If one falls down, his friend can help him up." (3:9–10)

"Whatever your hand finds to do, do with all your might." (9:10)

"Sow your seed in the morning, and at evening let not your hands be idle. For you do not know which will succeed, whether this or that or whether both will do equally well." (11:6)

"A fool's work wearies him." (10:15)

"Anyone who is among the living has hope." (9:4)

We lose what is valuable in [our personal relationships]—love, joy, communality—less through conflict and tragedy than through long series of shadowy and often unconscious refusals. Withdrawing, forgetting, falling out of touch, ignoring or avoiding or withholding the unpretentious but essentials of friendship destroy more relationships than death or anger and tend to isolate their perpetrators quite early in the solitary confinement of old age.

Robert Grudin, *Time and the Art of Living*

There are many occasions when the call to service can also provide for career advancement. As a post-doctoral student at Stanford University, Dave Altman created a health advocacy discussion group, at which the issue of tobacco disease came up as an instance where science could support the need for public policy change. This research led him to help establish STAT (Stop Teenage Addiction to Tobacco) as a nonprofit advocacy group. Today, he says that his advocacy work has had more influence on his research career than any other factor. He recently became an associate professor at the Bowman Gray Medical School, which ironically is named after the former CEO of the RJ Reynolds Tobacco Company. Altman says his work is highly rewarding, because it allows him to bring together research, action and ethics.

Look for opportunities to bring together your personal and work concerns. Abhay Bhushan was a strategic planner at Xerox Corp. in Palo Alto, California. After Earth Day 1990, he developed a proposal for a companywide initiative to deal with paper, chemicals and packaging. He received enthusiastic support from top management, and it has now become a full-time job.

In her book, *Making a Living while Making a Difference: A Guide to Careers with a Conscience,* Melissa Everett provides a wonderful discussion on commitment. "One of the most frightening aspects of commitment," she says, "is the specter of success. Because unconditional commitment to one's work is powerful, it's also terrifying—so terrifying that many of us screen it out of our awareness at all costs." True commitment, which she distinguishes from externally imposed duty, includes the following components:

> It comes from within, articulated by what's important in your life.

> Keeping such a commitment offers a path for self-expression and actualization. It may require delay of gratification, but not suppression of your essential self.

> It's grounded in a higher purpose than personal satisfaction; it entails the desire to leave a legacy.

Everett says that commitment isn't just a state of mind, but requires a consistent pattern of behavior. It's not just caring, but cultivating the skills necessary to effectively act upon that commitment.

Spiritual drives make us want to touch what is deepest, most hidden, in ourselves. The closer we come to this hidden core, the more certain we can be that our spirituality will emerge and direct us, and that we will come to see ourselves—and others—as fundamentally good or decent.

Marsha Sinetar, *Developing a 21st-Century Mind*

Max Lucado, in his book *He Still Moves Stones*, said "God honors radical risk-taking faith." Consider whether in your dreams you're thinking big enough. Could this be the time for you to take a radical leap of faith?

Faith without action is dead. Imagine what a waste it would be if the ultimate goal of being human was to avoid sin and nothing more. Service to others is the ultimate expression of the meaning of life. List five ways that you could help someone else this year.

Mother Theresa was once asked why she spent her time caring for the poor of Calcutta, knowing she could never be successful. "We're not here to be successful," she snapped. "We're here to be faithful." What needs might be met by your being faithful?

Slobodan Djurdjevic came to the United States from Yugoslavia in 1973 with his family. In this home country, he had been a successful businessman, but since he spoke no English, in this country all he could find was a job as a housekeeper. One day, when his depression had just about hit bottom, he read a story of a young woman who had written to her father of her own despair, ending by telling of her intention to take her own life. He responded with a story of the two men together in prison: one looked through the bars and saw only mud, the other looked out and saw stars. At that moment, Djurdjevic committed himself to seeing stars. He started working a second shift, began to take English lessons and today is a department manager at Abbott Laboratories in suburban Chicago.

Among all my patients in the second half of life—that is to say, over 35—there has not been one whose problem in the last resort was not that of finding a religious outlook on life . . . this of course has nothing whatever to do with a particular creed or membership of a church.

C. G. Jung

Santos Mora came to the United States from Mexico, where many of his family still live. He, too, is a manager of Abbott Laboratories. His family is poor, and so when his grandmother died, he agreed to pay for all funeral and travel expenses, though he didn't know just how he would do it. The day after he returned from the funeral in Mexico, he was called into his supervisor's office and given an unexpected performance bonus that covered all of the costs. Mora believes that you can't permanently give anything away—it will always come back to you with interest.

Is there a special cause about which you believe strongly? Maybe instead of chasing a job, you would find it more rewarding to change the world. Consider starting your own nonprofit organization. There are thousands of private and governmental funding sources for people and organizations that are trying to accomplish worthwhile goals. If you decide to take this route, be aware that it will probably take more time than you think to obtain tax-exempt status and entice donors to contribute to your cause.

What are the first things to go in school budget cuts? Typically, art, music and other "nonessential" courses. How sad!

Where else do children learn to be creative? Try to build artistic creativity into your home life—even if it's finger-painting, making collages or singing travel songs. Slowly, that creative spirit will flow over into your work.

Discovering and working on our mission in life is more than just doing what we love most and serving others as we do it. When we are working at our mission, we've entered a state of grace in which the Creator's love is flowing clearly through us. Only here will we find our true happiness.

Robert Roskind, *In the Spirit of Business*

Bob Pike took early retirement from a manufacturing company to self-publish and market a book he'd written teaching children to play checkers. A champion checker player himself, Pike believed that teaching young people to play the game could help pry them away from the TV and make connections with their parents. He now does demonstrations in libraries, schools and bookstores. (To order a copy of his book, *Winning Checkers for Kids of All Ages* call 800-642-6657.)

Coach, or assist the coach, for a youth athletic team. If you're not sure what to do, read *Positive Coaching: Building Character and Self-Esteem Through Sports* by Jim Thompson (at your bookstore, or call 800-699-2733).

What do these famous motivational writers and speakers have in common: Norman Vincent Peale *(The Power of Positive Thinking)*, Robert H. Schuller *(Tough Times Don't Last, Tough People Do)*, Mark Victor Hansen *(Chicken Soup for the Soul)* and Anthony Robbins *(Awaken the Giant Within)?* They, like many other great achievers, truly believe that one who gives receives back in greater measure, and have made giving a central part of their core personal philosophy. Whether you have a great or small income, increase your giving now. You'll be amazed at the unpredictable return on investment.

The foundational principles and the recognition of the four needs and capacities—to live, to love, to learn, to leave a legacy—are transcultural, transreligious, transnational, transracial. Regardless of who or where they are, when people get into their deep inner lives, they sense true north.

Stephen R. Covey, A. Roger Merrill, and
Rebecca R. Merrill, *First Things First*

Find somebody for whom you can be a guardian angel.

C. Everett Koop, M.D., is now well into his third career. During his first, he was one of the world's foremost pediatric surgeons. In his second, he served as U.S. Surgeon General, taking courageous stands on many public health issues, including tobacco control and AIDS. Now, at an age where many of his contemporaries are retired to the golf course or nursing home, Dr. Koop is working for reform of the health care delivery system, and to educate the public about the need to take personal responsibility for their own health. What drives this man? At root is a powerful faith that humans have been put on earth for a purpose, and an important part of that purpose is service to others.

African healer and drummer Onye Onyemaechi has a dream: to construct African villages in the United States as a place where young people can escape the violence and drugs in the environment of inner-city ghettos. At such a place, they could benefit from the wisdom of African spiritual roots, and learn from their wise elders. Matthew Fox, in his book *The Reinvention of Work*, cites Onyemaechi's dream as one example of how people can make a difference if they have vision and courage.

Imagine the pleasure that God must have felt in creating this world: the breathtaking awe of building great mountains; the unbridled laughter at watching a baby giraffe or an alarmed tree sloth; the heartwarming joy at seeing creation reenacted each time a new infant is born. Humans, the Bible tells us, were created in God's image. How can you experience God's pleasure through what you create in your work?

To understand man's significance, I say, you must first accept his insignificance. Only then could you focus him into importance against his stupendous, unshruggable background. And now, accepting this vision utterly, accepting it without fear and with joy, I had, for the time being at least, found all I needed.

Colin Fletcher, *The Man Who Walked Through Time*

Recall the parable of the man who buried his gold coin to keep it safe, and was reprimanded for not having wisely invested it to make it grow (Matthew, 25:14–30). Are there talents of your own being buried when they would better be cultivated and grown?

Indeed, make something of yourself, try your best to get to the top, if that's where you want to go, but know that the more people you try to take along with you, the faster you'll get there and the longer you'll stay there.

James A. Autry, *Love and Profit: The Art of Caring Leadership*

Pay careful attention to how your prayers are answered; the answers might not be what you expected or even wanted. In his collection of quirky short poems entitled *The Sound of One Hand Working,* McZen said:

> I pray for wisdom,
> am answered with a study guide.
> I pray for strength,
> am answered with an exercise routine.
> I pray for courage,
> am answered with a call to commitment.
> I pray for generalities,
> am answered with specifics.

Faith is not really faith until it's acted upon. Then it comes alive. It means something.

Millard and Linda Fuller, *The Excitement Is Building*

Richard Barrett, an engineer at the World Bank in Washington, DC, started a group that meets weekly for "spiritual unfoldment." The group now has more than 60 people participating, ranging from senior managers to junior staff. What can you do to spark a spiritual renaissance where you work?

Embrace the paradox inherent in the new world of work: failure can lead to success; the greatest risk can be in taking no risk, while the least risk can be in taking great risk; the best way to think big might be to think small; and the best way to make money might be not trying to make money but pursuing larger values.

A paradise of inward tranquillity seems to be faith's usual result; and it's easy, even without being religious oneself, to understand this . . . . How can it possibly fail to steady the nerves, to

*cool the fever and appease the fret, if one is sensibly conscious
that, no matter what one's difficulties for the moment may
appear to be, one's life as a whole is in the keeping of a power
whom one can absolutely trust?*

William James, *The Varieties of Religious Experience*

According to an article in *The Wall Street Journal,* Phil Hagans,
who owns a McDonald's franchise, has become "a one-man
social-service agency." Hagans hires inner-city youth, and then as-
sists them with financial planning, personal counseling and helping them with school. The same article quotes Reggie Webb, who
owns four McDonalds outlets near Los Angeles, as saying, "We're
teaching kids American values—the work ethic, showing up on
time, how to dress, the importance of working as a team." In your
work, what can you do for our young people?

After almost a year of unemployment, an Atlanta man left
town for a job in West Virginia. Unfortunately, he was unable
to find a home for his family or a suitable job for his wife. After
eight months of separation, he finally knew that he had to walk
away from a secure source of income to rejoin his family and
renew his job search in Atlanta. He landed a position working construction to make ends meet, and in every spare moment, he typed
letters and made phone calls. Within a month, he received an offer
for the best job he'd ever taken. Had he not had the faith to walk
away from a sure thing, he says, he would never have been able to
move forward.

If you decide to move into the nonprofit sector, don't think it will
be easy. In an *Inc.* magazine article entitled "The New Dog-Eat-
Dog Nonprofit," Donna Fenn described how Dave Hilliard had to
employ sophisticated strategic planning, financing and operating
procedures to assure the survival and success of the Wyman Center, a summer camp for disadvantaged youth. Hilliard concludes,

"We can manage ourselves with all the rigorous intensity of a business. It doesn't take a thing away from our mission."

The nonprofit world needs entrepreneurs. In one of his monthly columns in *Success* magazine, Wilson Harrell tells of Pride Industries in Roseville, California. Since 1983, the organization has grown from a budget of $400,000, mostly in government money, to more than $30 million, of which almost 90 percent comes from the sale of products and services. CEO Michael Ziglar's office is decorated with awards like Entrepreneur of the Year, Sacramento Businessman of the Year and others.

Watching the mentally and physically challenged employees at Pride, Harrell said, "was a ride on an emotional rollercoaster. I went from sympathy to the employees disabilities to admiration for their ingenuity, choking back tears of joy to see people so motivated and so happy." If you get a call from Michael Ziglar, Harrell concludes, he won't be begging for a handout, he'll be asking for your business . . . and doing God's work.

To learn more about opportunities in the nonprofit sector, contact ACCESS: Networking in the Public Interest at 202-785-4233. ACCESS publishes a monthly newspaper called *Community Jobs,* which includes articles, resource lists, book reviews and nonprofit job listings. The third issue each month of the *National Business Employment Weekly* includes advertisements from this publication for nonprofit jobs.

While 60–70 percent of employees consider a "code of values" either "very" or "somewhat" prevalent among business, only 7 percent think that most companies actually live by them.

William Morin, *Silent Sabotage*

Relationships that are based on mutual financial benefit tend to grow weaker in adversity, while relationships that are built on love and personal respect tend to grow stronger in adversity. What is the basis for your primary relationships?

Courage includes; fear excludes. Is your approach to life to include people in your circle, or to keep them out?

In his Pulitzer Prize-winning book *Leadership,* James MacGregor Burns wrote that the essence of transforming leadership is to provoke followers "to respond to the higher levels of moral development." What are you doing to help the moral development of those with whom you work?

Benevolence is expected at Tom's, which is why we put our money where our values are by encouraging employees to donate 5 percent of their time at work—for which we still pay them their usual wages—to community needs.

Tom Chappell, owner, Tom's of Maine, and
author of *The Soul of a Business*

Stay away from people with impure motives.

RECEIVE A FREE NBEW REPRINT BOOKLET:
"Before the Job Search"

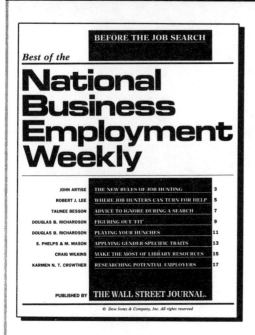

No matter where your career is headed, the *National Business Employment Weekly* points you in the direction of career success. As you begin your search for a new position, our "Before the Job Search" reprint booklet will help you better understand the challenges that await you. Its content reflects the care and preparation you'll find throughout each issue of the *National Business Employment Weekly*.